CHINA IN THE 21ST CENTURY

U.S.-CHINA TRADE

ISSUES AND PATTERNS

China in the 21st Century

Additional books in this series can be found on Nova's website under the Series tab.

Additional E-books in this series can be found on Nova's website under the E-book tab.

Trade Issues, Policies and Laws

Additional books in this series can be found on Nova's website under the Series tab.

Additional E-books in this series can be found on Nova's website under the E-book tab.

CHINA IN THE 21ST CENTURY

U.S.-CHINA TRADE

ISSUES AND PATTERNS

JOSEPHINE A. GONZALEZ
EDITOR

nova publishers
New York

For permission to use material from this book please contact us:
Telephone 631-231-7269; Fax 631-231-8175
Web Site: http://www.novapublishers.com

Additional color graphics may be available in the e-book version of this book.

Library of Congress Cataloging-in-Publication Data

ISBN: 978-1-62618-538-8

Published by Nova Science Publishers, Inc. † New York

Contents

PREFACE

U.S.-China economic ties have expanded substantially over the past three decades. Total U.S.-China trade rose from $5 billion in 1981 to an estimated $503 billion in 2011, and is projected to reach $539 billion in 2012. China is currently the United States' second-largest trading partner, its third-largest export market, and its biggest source of imports. Because U.S. imports from China have risen much more rapidly than U.S. exports to China, the U.S. merchandise trade deficit has grown from $10 billion in 1990 to $296 billion in 2011, and is projected to reach $311 billion in 2012. The rapid pace of economic integration between China and the U.S., while benefiting both sides overall, has made the trade relationship increasingly complex. This book provides an overview of U.S.-China trade relations, surveys major trade disputes, and lists bills introduced in Congress that could affect bilateral commercial ties.

Chapter 1 – U.S.-China economic ties have expanded substantially over the past three decades. Total U.S.- China trade rose from $5 billion in 1981 to an estimated $503 billion in 2011, and is projected to reach $539 billion in 2012. China is currently the United States' second-largest trading partner, its third-largest export market, and its biggest source of imports. Because U.S. imports from China have risen much more rapidly than U.S. exports to China, the U.S. merchandise trade deficit has grown from $10 billion in 1990 to $296 billion in 2011, and is projected to reach $311 billion in 2012. The rapid pace of economic integration between China and the United States, while benefiting both sides overall, has made the trade relationship increasingly complex. China's large population and booming economy have made it a large and growing market for U.S. exporters and investors. According to one estimate, China is currently a $250 billion market for U.S. firms (i.e., U.S. exports to

China plus sales by U.S.-invested firms in China). U.S. imports of low-cost goods from China greatly benefit U.S. consumers, and U.S. firms that use China as the final point of assembly for their products, or use Chinese-made inputs for production in the United States, are able to lower costs and become more globally competitive. China's purchases of U.S. Treasury securities (which total nearly $1.2 trillion) help keep U.S. interest rates low. On the other hand, many analysts argue that growing commercial ties with China have exposed many U.S. firms to greater competition from low-cost Chinese firms, which they contend has negatively affected wages and employment in a number of U.S. industries.

Despite implementing extensive economic and trade reforms over the past 30 years, China's transition to a free market economy remains incomplete. China continues to maintain, or has recently imposed, a number of distortive economic and trade policies. Such policies have increasingly strained commercial relations with China's trading partners, including the United States. Major concerns raised by U.S. policymakers and stakeholders include China's efforts to maintain an undervalued currency, its mixed record on implementing its World Trade Organization (WTO) obligations, its relatively poor record on protecting intellectual property rights (IPR), and its extensive use of industrial policies (such as financial support of state-owned firms, discriminatory government regulations, pressure on foreign-invested firms in China to transfer technology, and export restrictions on raw materials). Many analysts argue that such policies are harmful to U.S. economic interests and have contributed to U.S job losses. For example, one U.S. government study estimated that IPR infringement in China cost U.S. IPRintensive firms $48 billion in 2009.

Some Members of Congress advocate a more aggressive U.S. trade policy towards China, such as increasing the number of dispute settlement cases brought against China in the WTO, where the United States has prevailed on a number of issues. During his State of the Union Address in January 2012, President Obama announced plans to create a new Trade Enforcement Unit "charged with investigating unfair trade practices in countries like China." Some analysts caution that taking a more aggressive stance against China over its trade policies could induce it to retaliate against U.S. exports to, and investment in, China. They further contend that major economic disputes should be dealt with through established high-level bilateral dialogues, such as the Strategic & Economic Dialogue (S&ED) and the U.S.-China Joint Commission on Commerce and Trade (JCCT). Many trade observers contend that the United States should also continue to press China to rebalance its economic growth model by boosting domestic consumption and decreasing the country's reliance on exports for its economic growth. This chapter provides an overview of U.S.-China trade ties and major issues.

Chapter 2 – Following China's accession to the World Trade Organization (WTO) in December 2001, expectations were high that U.S. exports to China would increase due to reduced tariffs and increased market access. An examination of trade data from 2000 to 2011 demonstrates the following patterns in U.S.-China trade that have taken place in the decade since China's accession to the WTO:

1. U.S. exports to China have more than quintupled in value but are dwarfed by the surge of Chinese imports into the United States, resulting in a steadily growing bilateral trade deficit;
2. A dramatic rise in the levels of non-manufactured goods (particularly agricultural products, raw materials, and mined natural resource products) exported by U.S. producers to China, to the extent that there is now a U.S. trade surplus with China in non-manufactured goods;
3. A dramatic rise in imports of Chinese-made manufactured goods into the United States, and a significant decrease in U.S. exports of manufactured goods to China as a share of total exports;
4. A steady move up the value chain for Chinese imports into the United States – most noticeably in computers and consumer electronics. However, in this latter category China often serves as an assembly and export platform for multinational corporations of components manufactured elsewhere in world, a fact that may not be clearly reflected in trade statistics.

In: U.S.-China Trade: Issues and Patterns ISBN: 978-1-62618-538-8
Editor: Josephine A. Gonzalez

Chapter 1

CHINA-U.S. TRADE ISSUES*

Wayne M. Morrison

SUMMARY

U.S.-China economic ties have expanded substantially over the past three decades. Total U.S.- China trade rose from $5 billion in 1981 to an estimated $503 billion in 2011, and is projected to reach $539 billion in 2012. China is currently the United States' second-largest trading partner, its third-largest export market, and its biggest source of imports. Because U.S. imports from China have risen much more rapidly than U.S. exports to China, the U.S. merchandise trade deficit has grown from $10 billion in 1990 to $296 billion in 2011, and is projected to reach $311 billion in 2012. The rapid pace of economic integration between China and the United States, while benefiting both sides overall, has made the trade relationship increasingly complex. China's large population and booming economy have made it a large and growing market for U.S. exporters and investors. According to one estimate, China is currently a $250 billion market for U.S. firms (i.e., U.S. exports to China plus sales by U.S.-invested firms in China). U.S. imports of low-cost goods from China greatly benefit U.S. consumers, and U.S. firms that use China as the final point of assembly for their products, or use Chinese-made inputs for production in the United States, are able to lower costs and become more globally competitive. China's purchases of U.S. Treasury securities (which total nearly $1.2 trillion) help keep U.S. interest rates low. On the

---

* This is an edited, reformatted and augmented version of Congressional Research Service, Publication No. RL33536, dated November 29, 2012.

other hand, many analysts argue that growing commercial ties with China have exposed many U.S. firms to greater competition from low-cost Chinese firms, which they contend has negatively affected wages and employment in a number of U.S. industries.

Despite implementing extensive economic and trade reforms over the past 30 years, China's transition to a free market economy remains incomplete. China continues to maintain, or has recently imposed, a number of distortive economic and trade policies. Such policies have increasingly strained commercial relations with China's trading partners, including the United States.

Major concerns raised by U.S. policymakers and stakeholders include China's efforts to maintain an undervalued currency, its mixed record on implementing its World Trade Organization (WTO) obligations, its relatively poor record on protecting intellectual property rights (IPR), and its extensive use of industrial policies (such as financial support of state-owned firms, discriminatory government regulations, pressure on foreign-invested firms in China to transfer technology, and export restrictions on raw materials). Many analysts argue that such policies are harmful to U.S. economic interests and have contributed to U.S job losses.

For example, one U.S. government study estimated that IPR infringement in China cost U.S. IPRintensive firms $48 billion in 2009.

Some Members of Congress advocate a more aggressive U.S. trade policy towards China, such as increasing the number of dispute settlement cases brought against China in the WTO, where the United States has prevailed on a number of issues. During his State of the Union Address in January 2012, President Obama announced plans to create a new Trade Enforcement Unit "charged with investigating unfair trade practices in countries like China."

Some analysts caution that taking a more aggressive stance against China over its trade policies could induce it to retaliate against U.S. exports to, and investment in, China.

They further contend that major economic disputes should be dealt with through established high-level bilateral dialogues, such as the Strategic & Economic Dialogue (S&ED) and the U.S.-China Joint Commission on Commerce and Trade (JCCT). Many trade observers contend that the United States should also continue to press China to rebalance its economic growth model by boosting domestic consumption and decreasing the country's reliance on exports for its economic growth.

This chapter provides an overview of U.S.-China trade ties and major issues.

Introduction

Economic and trade reforms begun in 1979 have helped transform China into one of the world's fastest-growing economies. China's economic growth and trade liberalization, including comprehensive trade commitments made upon entering the World Trade Organization (WTO) in 2001, have led to a sharp expansion in U.S.-China commercial ties. Yet, bilateral trade relations have become increasingly strained in recent years over a number of issues, including a large and growing U.S. trade deficit with China, resistance by China to reforming its currency policy, U.S. concerns over China's mixed record on implementing its WTO obligations, and numerous Chinese industrial policies that appear to impose new restrictions on foreign firms. Several Members of Congress have called on the Obama Administration to take a tougher stance against China to induce it to eliminate economic policies deemed harmful to U.S. economic interests and/or inconsistent with WTO rules. This report provides an overview of U.S.-China trade relations, surveys major trade disputes, and lists bills introduced in Congress that could affect bilateral commercial ties.

Most Recent Developments

On September 28, 2012, President Obama issued an executive order requiring a Chinese-owned company to divest its interest in wind farm project companies in Oregon that it acquired earlier in the year, due to national security concerns.

On September 17, 2012, the USTR announced that it had initiated a WTO dispute settlement case against China over its export subsidies to auto and auto parts manufacturers in China.

On July 16, 2012, the USTR announced that the United States had prevailed in a WTO dispute settlement case regarding China's discrimination against U.S. suppliers of electronic payment services.

On July 5, 2012, the USTR initiated a WTO dispute settlement case against China over its imposition of antidumping and countervailing duties on more than $3 billion in U.S. auto exports to China.

On May 4, 2012, the United States and China concluded the fourth round of discussions held under the Strategic and Economic Dialogue (S&ED).

China pledged to continue its efforts to rebalance its economy and to increase foreign access to certain financial services.

On March 13, 2012, the United States, Japan, and the European Union jointly initiated a WTO dispute resolution case against China over its export restrictions on rare earths (as well as tungsten and molybdenum).

During the visit to the United States by Chinese Vice President Xi Jinping (February 13-17, 2012), China agreed that it would expand market access for American movies, open up its mandatory third-party liability insurance sector for autos to foreign firms, and hold bilateral talks on establishing international guidelines for export financing.

On January 30, 2012, a WTO Appellate Body ruled that China's export quotas and duties on certain raw materials were inconsistent with its WTO obligations. The case was originally brought by the United States in 2009.

During his State of the Union Address on January 24, 2012, President Obama announced that he would create a new federal Trade Enforcement Unit "charged with investigating unfair trade practices in countries like China." On February 28, 2012, President Obama issued an executive order establishing an Interagency Trade Enforcement Center within the USTR's office.

U.S. TRADE WITH CHINA[1]

U.S.-China trade rose rapidly after the two nations reestablished diplomatic relations (in January 1979), signed a bilateral trade agreement (July 1979), and provided mutual most-favored-nation (MFN) treatment beginning in 1980.[2] In 1979 (when China's economic reforms began), total U.S.-China trade (exports plus imports) was $2 billion; China ranked as the United States' 23rd-largest export market and its 45th-largest source of imports. In 2012, total bilateral trade is projected to reach $539 billion. China is currently the second-largest U.S. trading partner (after Canada), the third-largest U.S. export market (after Canada and Mexico), and the largest source of U.S. imports. In recent years, China has been one of the fastest-growing U.S. export markets, and the importance of this market is expected to grow even further, given the pace of China's economic growth, and as Chinese living standards continue to improve and a sizable Chinese middle class emerges. According to one estimate, China is currently a $250 billion market for U.S. firms (this includes U.S. exports to China plus sales by U.S.-invested firms in China).[3]

A major concern among many U.S. policymakers has been the surge in the U.S. trade deficit with China over the past two decades, as U.S. imports from

China have grown much faster than U.S. exports to China. The U.S. merchandise trade deficit with China rose from $10 billion in 1990 to $266 billion in 2008; it fell to $227 billion in 2009 (due largely to the effects of the global economic downturn that began in 2008), then rose to $273 billion in 2010 and to $296 billion in 2011. The U.S. trade deficit with China is projected to reach $311 billion in 2012 (see Table 1 and Figure 1).[4]

For the past several years, the U.S. trade deficit with China has been significantly larger than that with any other U.S. trading partner and several trading groups. As can be seen in Figure 2, the U.S. trade deficit with China in 2011 was larger than the combined U.S. trade deficits with the Organization of the Petroleum Exporting Countries (OPEC), the 27 nations that make up the European Union (EU27), and the 10 nations that make up the Association of Southeast Asian Nations (ASEAN).

Some Members contend that the large U.S. trade deficit is an indicator that the trade relationship is unbalanced, unfair, and damaging to the U.S. economy.

In the 112th Congress, H.R. 2909 (Sherman) would terminate China's normal trade relations status and would direct the President to negotiate a new trade agreement with China in order to achieve a balance of trade in four years.

Table 1. U.S. Merchandise Trade with China: 1980-2011and Projections for 2012 ($ billions)

Year	U.S. Exports	U.S. Imports	U.S. Trade Balance
1980	3.8	1.1	2.7
1985	3.9	3.9	0.0
1990	4.8	15.2	-10.4
1995	11.7	45.6	-33.8
2000	16.3	100.1	-83.8
2005	41.8	243.5	-201.6
2006	55.2	287.8	-232.5
2007	65.2	321.5	-256.3
2008	71.5	337.8	-266.3
2009	69.6	296.4	-226.8
2010	91.9	364.9	-273.1
2011	103.9	393.3	-295.5
2012 (projected)	114.1	425.3	-311.2

Source: U.S. International Trade Commission (USITC) DataWeb.

Note: Data for 2012 are projections based on actual data for January-September 2012.

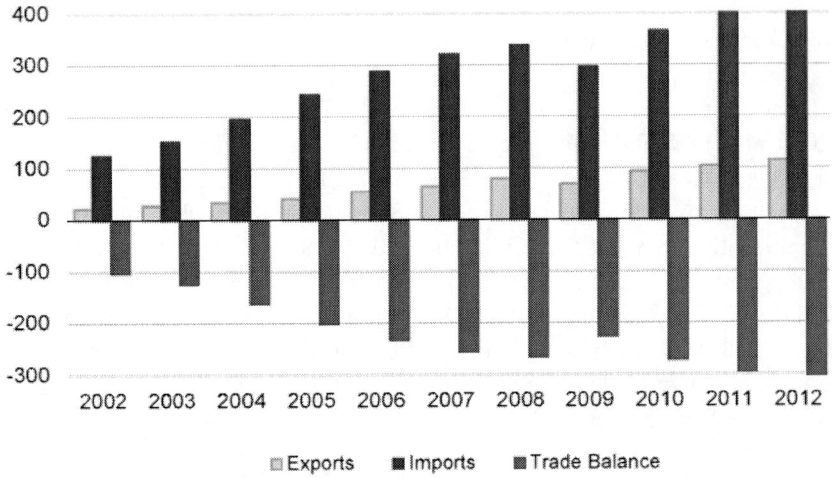

Source: U.S. International Trade Commission
Note: Data for 2012 are projections, based on actual data for January-September 2012.

Figure 1. U.S. Merchandise Trade with China: 2002-2011 and Projections for 2012; ($ billions).

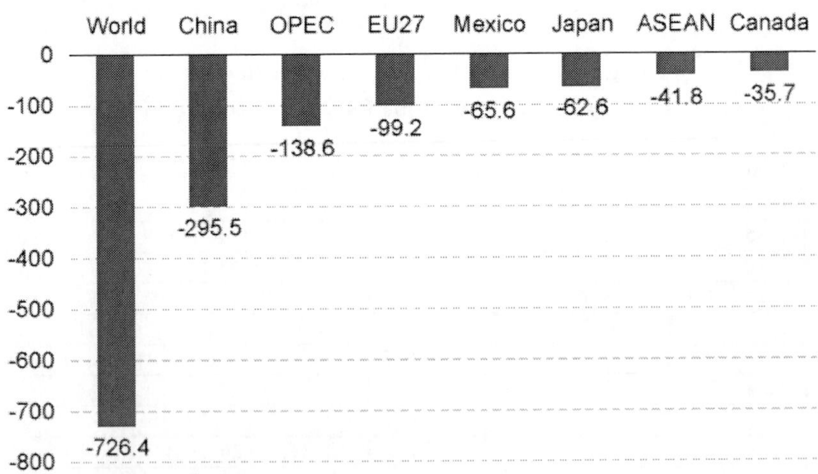

Source: U.S. International Trade Commission DataWeb.

Figure 2. U.S. Trade Balances with Selected Trading Partners: 2011; ($ billions).

U.S. Merchandise Exports to China

U.S. merchandise exports to China in 2011 were $103.9 billion, up 13.1% over 2010 levels.[5] China replaced Japan as the third-largest U.S. merchandise export market in 2007 and has remained so through the present (see Figure 3). From 2000 to 2011, the share of total U.S. exports going to China rose from 2.1% to 7.0%.[6] U.S. exports to China are projected rise to rise to $114.1 billion in 2012, up 5.8% over the previous year. The top five merchandise U.S. exports to China in 2011 were waste and scrap, oilseeds and grains, aircraft and parts, semiconductors and other electronic components, and motor vehicles (see Table 2).

China is also a significant market for U.S. exports of private services. These totaled $26.7 billion in 2011 (the most recent year available), a 26.5% increase over 2010 levels, making China the fifth-largest export market for U.S. private services.

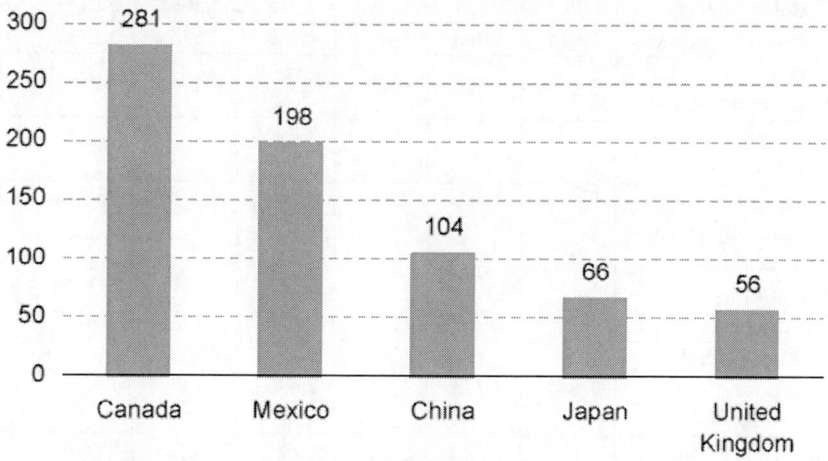

Source: U.S. International Trade Commission DataWeb.

Figure 3. Top 5 U.S. Export Markets: 2011; ($ billions).

Although U.S. exports to China slowed somewhat in 2011 relative to previous years (and compared with the growth in U.S. exports to other major trading partners), when measured over a 10-year period, China has been by far one of the fastest-growing U.S. export markets, as seen in Table 3. From 2002 to 2011, U.S. exports to China increased by about 471% (the overall growth in U.S. exports over this period was 213.6%).[7]

Table 2. Major U.S. Exports to China: 2007-2011 ($ millions and percent change)

NAIC Commodity	2007	2008	2009	2010	2011	2010-2011 Percent Change
Total Exports to China	65,238	71,457	69,576	91,878	103,879	13.1%
Waste and scrap	7,331	7,562	7,142	8,561	11,540	34.8%
Oilseeds and grains	4,145	7,316	9,376	11,208	11,500	2.6%
Aerospace products and parts	7,447	5,471	5,344	5,766	6,392	10.9%
Semiconductors and other electronic components	7,435	7,475	6,041	7,555	5,668	-25.0%
Motor vehicles	908	1,194	1,134	3,515	5,369	52.7%
Basic chemicals	2,914	3,090	3,433	4,202	4,658	10.8%
Resin, synthetic rubber, & artificial	3,290	3,524	4,036	4,336	4,476	3.2%
& synthetic fibers & filament						
Navigational, measuring,electro-medical, and control instruments	2,444	2,886	2,917	3,782	4,275	13.0%
Other general purpose machinery	1,885	2,273	1,890	2,445	3,113	27.3%
Other agricultural products	1,558	1,786	1,008	2,328	2,825	21.4%

Source: USITC DataWeb.

Note: Top 10 U.S. exports to China in 2011using the North American Industry Classification (NAIC) System on a 4-digit level.

Many trade analysts argue that China could prove to be a much more significant market for U.S. exports in the future. China is one of the world's fastest-growing economies, and rapid economic growth is likely to continue in the near future, provided that economic reforms are continued.[8] China's goals of modernizing its infrastructure, upgrading its industries, and improving rural living standards could generate substantial demand for foreign goods and services. Finally, economic growth has substantially improved the purchasing power of Chinese citizens, especially those living in urban areas along the east coast of China.

Table 3. Major U.S. Merchandise Export Markets in 2011 ($ billions and percent change)

	2002	2010	2011	2010-2011 Percent Change	2002-2011 Percent Change
Total Global U.S. Exports	693.3	1,277.5	1,480.6	15.9%	213.6%
Canada	160.8	248.2	280.8	13.1%	174.6%
Mexico	97.5	163.3	197.5	21.0%	202.5%
China	22.1	91.9	103.9	13.1%	471.0%
Japan	51.4	60.5	66.2	9.3%	128.6%
United Kingdom	33.3	48.5	56.0	15.4%	168.3%
Germany	26.6	48.2	49.1	1.9%	184.5%
Korea	22.6	38.8	43.5	12.0%	192.5%
Brazil	12.4	35.4	42.9	21.5%	346.1%
Netherlands	18.3	35.0	42.8	22.4%	233.6%
Hong Kong	12.6	26.6	36.5	37.4%	289.5%

Source: U.S. International Trade Commission DataWeb.

China's growing economy, large foreign exchange reserves (at over $3.2 trillion as of December 2011), and large population of over 1.3 billion people make it a potentially enormous market. To illustrate:

- According to a report by the Boston Consulting Group, in 2009, China had 148 million "middle class and affluent" consumers, defined as those whose annual household income was 60,000 RMB ($9,160) or higher, and that level is projected to rise to 415 million by 2020.[9] According to Bloomberg News, China had an estimated 1.1 million millionaires (converted to U.S. dollars) in 2010.[10]
- Although Chinese private consumption as a percent of GDP is much lower than that of most other major economies, the rate of growth of Chinese private consumption has been rising rapidly. For example, private consumption as a percent of GDP in China in 2011 was 34.0%, compared to 71.1% in the United States. However, the annual

rate of growth in Chinese private consumption from 2002 to 2011 averaged 8.0%, while the U.S. annual average was 1.9%.

- China's government has indicated that it plans to step up efforts to boost domestic spending to help lessen its dependence on exports as the major contributor to China's economic growth. In 2008, China began the implementation of a $586 billion economic stimulus package, largely focused on infrastructure projects. China's goals of developing its western regions, expanding and modernizing its infrastructure, boosting its social safety net (such as health care and pensions), modernizing and developing key industries, reducing pollution, and raising incomes of the rural poor will likely result in large-scale government spending levels.[11] China's 12th Five-Year Plan (2011- 2015) reportedly will allocate $1 trillion in infrastructure spending.
- China currently has the world's largest mobile phone network and one of the fastest-growing markets, with over 1 billion mobile phone subscribers as of March 2012, up from 87 million subscribers in 2000.[12]
- Boeing Corporation predicts that over the next 20 years (2011-2030), China will buy 5,000 new commercial airplanes valued at $600 billion and will be Boeing's largest commercial airplane customer outside the United States.[13]
- China replaced the United States as the world's largest Internet user in 2008. At the end of December 2011, China had an estimated 513 million users versus 245 million in the United States.[14] Yet, the percentage of the Chinese population using the Internet is small relative to the United States: 38.4% versus 78.3%, respectively.
- According to *Global Insight*, China reportedly overtook Japan in 2009 to become the largest producer of light vehicles (cars and light trucks) at 12.9 million units and overtook the United States as the global leader in sales of light vehicles at 13.0 million units.[15] China's light vehicle sales nearly doubled from 2008 to 2010 (due largely to government tax subsidies and incentives that were implemented in response to the global economic slowdown). By 2021, sales of light vehicles in China are projected to reach 31.5 million units, which would be nearly double the projected sales in the United States. The number of cars on the road in China rose from 14 million units in 2005 to an estimated 55.9 million units in 2011, and is projected to

reach 131.6 million by 2016, a level that would equal 96.1% of the projected number of cars on the road in the United States.[16]

- For the first time in its history, General Motors (GM) in 2010 sold more cars and trucks in China (at 2.35 million units) than it did in the United States (2.21 million units).[17] In 2011, GM sold 2.55 million vehicles in China (up 8.3% over 2010 levels) versus 2.50 million in the United States. GM in China currently has 11 joint ventures and two wholly owned foreign enterprises and employs more than 35,000 workers.[18]

Major U.S. Imports from China

China was the largest source of U.S. merchandise imports in 2011, at $399.3 billion. U.S. imports from China increased by 9.4% in 2011 (compared to 23.1% rise in 2010) over the previous year. China's share of total U.S. imports rose from 8.2% in 2000 to 19.1% in 2010, but dropped to 18.1% in 2011. The importance (ranking) of China as a source of U.S. imports has risen sharply, from eighth largest in 1990, to fourth in 2000, to second in 2004-2006, to first in 2007-2012. The top five U.S. imports from China in 2011 were computer equipment, communications equipment, miscellaneous manufactured products (such as toys and games), apparel, and semiconductors and other electronic parts (see Table 4). From January to September 2012, U.S. imports from China were up 6.5% over the same period in 2011. China was the 10th-largest source of private services imports at $11.3 billion in 2011.

Throughout the 1980s and 1990s, nearly all U.S. imports from China were low-value, labor-intensive products, such as toys and games, consumer electronic products, footwear, and textiles and apparel. However, over the past few years, an increasing proportion of U.S. imports from China have been comprised of more technologically advanced products (see text box below).

U.S.-China Trade in Advance Technology Products

According to the U.S. Census Bureau, U.S. imports of "advanced technology products" (ATP) from China in 2011 totaled $129.5 billion. ATP products accounted for 32.4% of total U.S. imports from China, compared with 19.2% ($29.3 billion) in 2003. In addition, ATP imports from China accounted for 33.5% of total U.S ATP imports (compared with 14.1% in 2003).

U.S. ATP exports to China in 2011 were $21.4 billion; these accounted for 20.6% of total U.S. exports to China and 7.5% of U.S. global ATP exports. In comparison, U.S. ATP exports to China in 2003 were $8.3 billion, which accounted for 29.2% of U.S. exports to China and 4.6% of total U.S. ATP exports.

The United States ran a $108.1 billion deficit in its ATP trade with China in 2011, up from a $21.0 billion deficit in 2003. Some see the large and growing U.S. trade deficit in ATP with China as a source of concern, contending that it signifies the growing international competitiveness of China in high technology. Others dispute this, noting that a large share of the ATP imports from China are in fact relatively low-end technology products and parts, such as notebook computers, or are products that are assembled in China using imported high technology parts that are largely developed and/or made elsewhere.

Table 4. Major U.S. Imports From China: 2007-2011 ($ millions and percent change)

NAIC Commodity	2007	2008	2009	2010	2011	2010-2011 Percent Change
Computer equipment	44,462	45,820	44,818	59,800	68,276	14.2%
Communications equipment	23,192	26,618	26,362	33,464	39,806	19.0%
Miscellaneous manufactured commodities	34,827	35,835	30,668	34,168	32,672	-4.4%
Apparel	22,955	22,583	22,669	26,603	27,554	3.6%
Semiconductors and other electronic components	15,353	13,645	12,363	18,263	19,835	8.6%
Footwear	13,929	14,230	13,119	15,673	16,482	5.2%
Audio and video equipment	19,075	19,715	18,253	19,493	15,853	-18.7%
Household and institutional furniture and kitchen cabinets	11,872	11,086	9,128	11,123	11,398	2.5%
Household appliances and miscellaneous machines	8,266	8,520	7,724	9,090	9,569	5.3%
Other fabricated metal products	6,781	7,242	5,690	7,228	8,638	19.5%
Total imports from China	321,508	337,790	296,402	364,944	399,335	9.4%

Source: U.S. International Trade Commission DataWeb.

Notes: Top 10 U.S. imports from China in 2011 using the North American Industry Classification (NAIC) System on a 4-digit level.

China as a Major Center for Global Supply Chains

Many analysts contend that the sharp increase in U.S. imports from China (and hence the growing bilateral trade imbalance) is largely the result of movement in production facilities from other (primarily Asian) countries to China. That is, various products that used to be made in such places as Japan, Taiwan, Hong Kong, etc., and then exported to the United States, are now being made in China (in many cases, by foreign firms in China). To illustrate, in 1990, 47.1% of the value of U.S. manufactured imports came from Pacific Rim countries (including China).[19] In 2011, Pacific Rim countries accounted for 46.1% of total U.S. manufactured imports. Over the same period, the share of total U.S. manufactured imports that came from China increased from 3.6% to 25.3%. In other words, while China was becoming an increasingly important source for U.S. manufactured imports, the relative importance of the rest of the Pacific Rim (as a whole) as a source of U.S. imports was declining, in part because many multinational firms were shifting their export-oriented manufacturing facilities to China (see Figure 4).[20]

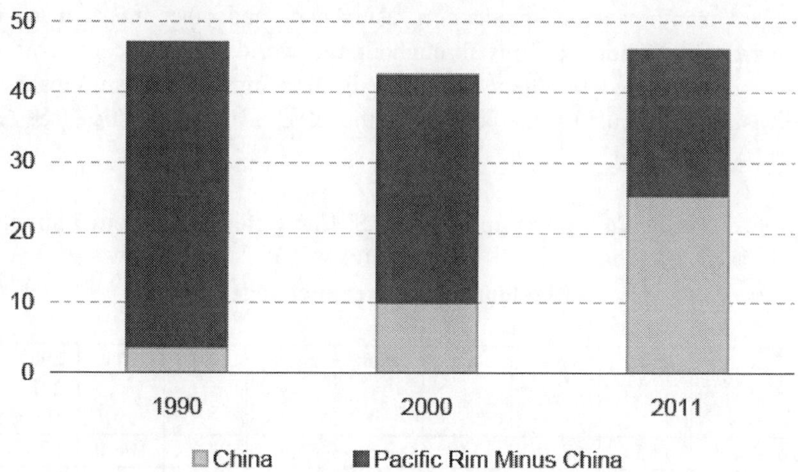

Source: U.S. International Trade Commission DataWeb.

Notes: Standard International Trade Classification (SITC) definition of manufactured imports.

Figure 4. U.S. Manufactured Imports from Pacific Rim Countries as a Percent of Total U.S. Manufactured Imports: 1990, 2000, and 2011.

Another illustration of the shift in production can be seen in the case of U.S. computer equipment imports, which constitute the largest category of U.S. imports from China (on an NAIC basis, 4- digit level). Table 5 lists U.S. imports of computer equipment and parts from 2000-2011. In 2000, Japan was the largest foreign supplier of U.S. computer equipment (with a 19.6% share of total U.S. imports), while China ranked fourth (with a 12.1% share). By 2011, Japan's ranking had fallen to third; the value of its shipments dropped by 61.9% over 2000 levels, and its share of U.S. computer imports declined to 4.8% (2011). China was by far the largest foreign supplier of computer equipment in 2011 with a 64.4% share of total U.S. computer equipment imports, compared to 12.0% in 2000 (see Figure 5). While U.S. imports of computer equipment from China from 2000-2011 rose by 722.9%, the total value of U.S. computer imports worldwide rose by 57.7%.[21] A study by the U.S. International Trade Commission (USITC) estimated that in 2002 over 99% of computer exports in China were from foreign-invested firms in China.[22] Taiwan, one of the world's leaders in sales of information technology, produces over 90% its information hardware equipment (such as computers) in China. Computer equipment, like many other globally traded products, often involves many stages of production, using parts and other inputs made by numerous multinational firms throughout the world, a significant share of which is assembled in China. The globalization of supply chains makes it increasingly difficult to interpret conventional U.S. trade statistics (see text box).

Table 5. Major Foreign Suppliers of U.S. Computer Equipment Imports: 2000-2011
($ billions and percent change)

	2000	**2002**	**2004**	**2006**	**2008**	**2010**	**2011**	**2000-2011 % change**
Total	68.5	62.3	73.9	83.8	85.4	97.2	106.0	57.7%
China	**8.3**	**12.0**	**29.5**	**40.0**	**45.8**	**59.8**	**68.3**	**722.9%**
Mexico	6.9	7.9	7.4	6.6	6.2	13.6	14.5	110.1%
Japan	13.4	8.1	6.3	6.3	6.6	5.2	5.1	-61.9%
Singapore	8.7	7.1	6.6	5.6	4.0	3.6	3.2	-63.2%
Thailand	2.4	2.1	2.3	3.2	3.7	3.5	3.0	25.0%

Source: U.S. International Trade Commission Trade DataWeb.

Note: Ranked according to top five foreign suppliers of computer equipment imports in 2011.

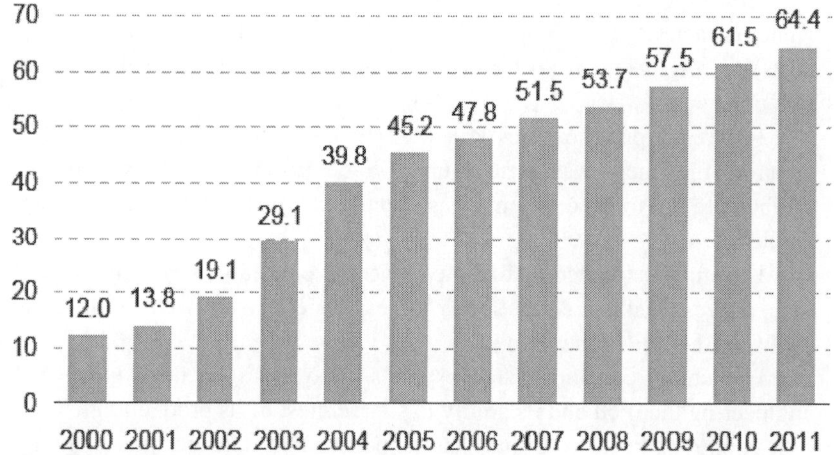

Source: U.S. International Trade Commission DataWeb.

Figure 5. U.S. Computer Imports from China as a Percent of U.S. Total Computer Imports: 2000-201 1 (%).

Global Supply Chains, China, and the Apple iPod: Who Benefits?

Many U.S. companies sign contracts with Taiwanese firms to have their products manufactured (mainly in China), and then shipped to the United States where they are sold by U.S. firms under their own brand name. In many instances, the level of value-added that occurs in China (often it simply involves assemblage) can be quite small relative to the overall cost/price of the final product.

One study by researchers at the University of California looked at the production of a 2005 Apple 30 gigabyte video iPod, which is made in China by Foxconn, a Taiwanese company, using parts produced globally (mainly in Asia).

The study estimated that it cost about $144 to make each iPod unit. Of this amount, only about $4, or 2.8% of the total cost, was attributable to the Chinese workers who assembled it; the rest of the costs were attributable to the numerous firms involved in making the parts (for example, Japanese firms provided the highest-value components—the hard drive and the display).[23]

From a trade aspect, U.S. trade data would have recorded the full value of each iPod unit imported from China at $144 (excluding shipping costs) as originating from China, even though the value added in China was quite small.

The retail price of the iPod sold in the United States was $299, meaning that there was a mark-up of about $155 per unit, which was attributable to transportation costs, retail and distributor margins, and Apple's profits.

The study estimated that Apple earned at least $80 on each unit it sold in its stores, making it the single largest beneficiary (in terms of gross profit) of the sale of the iPod.

The study concluded that Apple's innovation in developing and engineering the iPod and its ability to source most of its production to low-cost countries, such as China, has helped enable it to become a highly competitive and profitable firm (as well as a source for high-paying jobs in the United States).

The iPod example illustrates that the rapidly changing nature of global supply chains has made it increasing difficult to interpret the implications of U.S. trade data. Such data may show where products are being imported from, but they often fail to reflect who benefits from that trade. Chinese trade data indicate that over 50% of its exports are generated by foreign-invested firms in China.

Thus, in many instances, U.S. imports from China are really imports from many countries.

China's Tariff Schedule

China has significantly reduced its tariffs over the past three decades. China's simple average most-favored nation (MFN) applied tariff rate fell from around 50% in the early 1980s, to 15.6% in 2001, and to 9.6% in 2010.[24]

However, some U.S. policymakers complain that U.S. exporters to China face much higher tariff rates than do Chinese exporters to the United States. For example, as indicated in Table 6, China's simple average MFN applied tariff rate in 2010 was 174% higher than the U.S. rate of 3.5%. Such large differences in tariff rates exist across broad product categories.

For example, China's tariff rate on passenger vehicles (25%) was 10 times higher than the U.S. level (2.5%). Imported products into China are also subject to a value-added tax, which ranges from 5% to 17%.[25]

Table 6. Comparison of Chinese and U.S. Simple Average MFN Tariff Rates in 2010 (%)

	China	U.S.
Overall Average Applied MFN Rate	9.6	3.5
Animal products	14.8	2.3
Dairy products	12.0	20.3
Fruit, vegetables, plants	14.8	4.9
Coffee, tea	14.7	3.2
Cereals & preparations	24.3	3.5
Oilseeds, fats & oils	11.0	4.6
Sugars and confectionery	27.4	10.3
Beverages & tobacco	22.3	15.6
Cotton	15.2	4.1
Other agricultural products	11.4	1.1
Fish & fish products	10.9	1.0
Minerals & metals	7.4	1.7
Petroleum	4.8	1.4
Chemicals	6.6	2.8
Wood, paper, etc.	4.4	0.5
Textiles	9.6	7.9
Clothing	16.0	11.7
Leather, footwear, etc.	13.2	3.9
Non-electrical machinery	8.0	1.2
Electrical machinery	8.3	1.7
Transport equipment	11.5	3.0
Passenger Vehicles	25.0	2.5
Other Manufactures	11.9	2.4

Source: WTO World Tariff Profiles, 2011.

Note: Imports into China are also subject to a value-added tax; the standard rate is 17%.

U.S.-China Investment Ties[26]

Investment plays a large and growing role in U.S.-China commercial ties.[27] China's investment in U.S. assets can be broken down into several categories, including holdings of U.S. securities, foreign direct investment (FDI), and other non-bond investments. A significant share of China's investment in the United States is comprised of U.S. securities, while FDI constitutes the bulk of U.S. investment in China. The Treasury Department defines foreign holdings of U.S. securities as "U.S. securities owned by foreign residents (including banks and other institutions) except where the owner has a direct investment relationship with the U.S. issuer of the securities." U.S. statutes define FDI as "the ownership or control, directly or indirectly, by one foreign resident of 10% or more of the voting securities of an incorporated U.S. business enterprise or the equivalent interest in an unincorporated U.S. business enterprise, including a branch."[28] The U.S. Bureau of Economic Analysis (BEA) reports data on FDI flows to and from the United States.[29] China has also invested in a number of U.S. companies, projects, and various ventures which do meet the U.S. definition of FDI, and thus, are not reflected in BEA's data.

China's Holdings of U.S. Securities[30]

China's holdings of U.S. public and private securities are significant.[31] These include U.S. Treasury securities, U.S. government agency (such as Freddie Mac and Fannie Mae) securities, corporate securities, and equities (such as stocks). China's large holdings of U.S. securities can be largely attributed to its policy of intervening in exchange rate markets to limit the appreciation of its currency to the U.S. dollar (discussed in more detail below). For example, the Chinese government requires Chinese exporters (who are often paid in dollars) to turn over their dollars in exchange for Chinese currency. As a result, the Chinese government has accumulated a significant amount of dollars.[32] Rather than holding onto U.S. dollars, which earn no interest, the Chinese government has chosen to invest many of them into U.S. Treasury securities because they are seen as a relatively safe investment.[33] China's investment in public and private U.S. securities totaled $1,727 billion as of June 2011, up from $181 billion in 2002.

U.S. Treasury securities, which help the federal government finance its budget deficit, are the largest category of U.S. securities held by China.[34] As indicated in Table 7 and Figure 6, China's holdings of U.S. Treasury securities increased from $118 billion in 2002 to $1,152 billion in 2011 (year-end), making China the largest foreign holder of U.S. Treasury securities (it overtook Japan as the largest holder in 2008). China's holdings of U.S. Treasury securities in 2011 were down 0.7% over the previous year. As of September 2012, China's holdings of Treasury securities were $1,156 billion; these were up $300 million over August 2012 levels. However, the September 2012 level for China's holdings was $115 billion smaller than it was in September 2011 ($1,270 billion). Thus, China's holdings appear to be on the decline.[35] China's holdings of U.S. Treasury securities as a share of total foreign holdings rose from 9.6% in 2002 to 26.1% in 2010 (yearend), then declined to 23% in 2011 and to 21.2% as of September 2012.

Table 7. China's Holdings of U.S. Treasury Securities: 2002- September 2012

	2002	**2004**	**2006**	**2008**	**2010**	**2011**	**September 2012**
China's Holdings ($ billions)	118.0	222.9	396.9	727.4	1,160.1	1,151.9	1,155,6
China's Holdings as a Percent of Total Foreign Holdings	9.6%	12.1%	18.9%	23.6%	26.1%	23.0%	21.2%

Source: U.S. Treasury Department, year-end or month-end data.

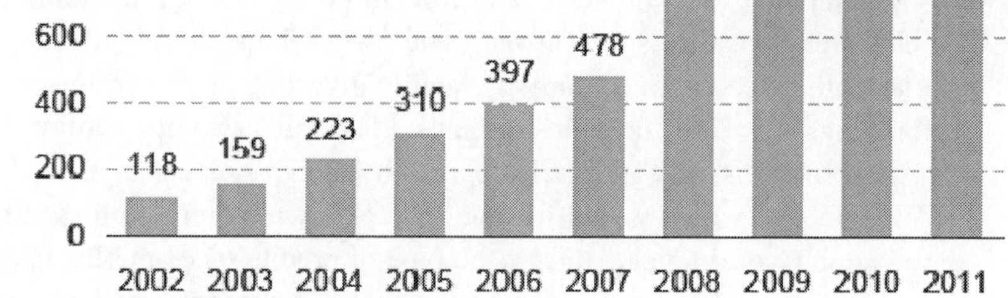

Source: U.S. Department of the Treasury.

Figure 6. China's Holdings of U.S. Treasury Securities: 2002-2011 (year-end); ($ billions).

Some analysts have raised concerns that China's large holdings of U.S. debt securities could give China leverage over U.S. foreign policy, including trade policy. They argue, for example, China might attempt to sell (or threaten to sell) a large share of its U.S. debt securities as punishment over a policy dispute, which could damage the U.S. economy. Others counter that China's holdings of U.S. debt give it very little practical leverage over the United States. They argue that, given China's economic dependency on a stable and growing U.S. economy, and its substantial holdings of U.S. securities, any attempt to try to sell a large share of those holdings would likely damage both the U.S. and Chinese economies. Such a move could also cause the U.S. dollar to sharply depreciate against global currencies, which could reduce the value of China's remaining holdings of U.S. dollar assets. Analysts also note that, while China is the largest foreign owner of U.S. Treasury Securities, those holdings are equal to only 8.6% of total U.S. public debt (FY2011). Finally, it is argued that, as long as China continues to largely peg the RMB to the U.S. dollar, it has little choice but to purchase U.S. dollar assets in order to maintain that peg. Legislation has been introduced in the 112th Congress that would seek to assess the implications for the United States of China's ownership of U.S. debt.

- H.R. 2166 (Sam Johnson) and S. 1028 (Cornyn), both titled "Foreign-Held Debt Transparency and Threat Assessment Act," would seek to increase the transparency of foreign ownership of U.S. debt instruments, especially in regard to China, in order to better assess the potential risks such holdings could pose for the United States. The bills state, for example, that under certain circumstances, China's holdings of U.S. debt could give it a tool with which it can try to manipulate U.S. domestic and foreign policymaking, including the U.S. relationship with Taiwan; and that China could attempt to destabilize the U.S. economy by rapidly divesting large portions of its holdings of U.S. debt instruments. The bills would require the President to issue a quarterly report on foreign holders of U.S. debt instruments, which would include a breakdown of foreign ownership by country of domicile and by the type of creditor (i.e., public, quasi-public, private); an analysis of the country's purpose and long-term intentions in regard to its U.S. debt holdings; an analysis of the current and foreseeable risks to U.S. national security and economic stability of each nation's U.S. debt holdings; and a determination whether such risks are "acceptable or unacceptable." If the President determined that a foreign country's holdings of U.S. debt instruments were an unacceptable risk, he would be required to formulate an action plan to reduce that risk.

- H.R. 1540 (McKeon) would, among other things, require the Secretary of Defense to conduct a national security risk assessment of U.S. federal debt held by China.[36] In addition, the Director of the Congressional Budget Office would be required to determine, and make publicly available, the amount of accrued interest on U.S. federal debt paid to China during the past five years.
- The conference report accompanying the National Defense Authorization Act of FY2012 (H.R. 1540, P.L. 112-81) included a provision requiring the Secretary of Defense to conduct a national security risk assessment of U.S. federal debt held by China. The Secretary of Defense issued a report in July 2012, stating that "attempting to use U.S. Treasury securities as a coercive tool would have limited effect and likely would do more harm to China than to the United States." As the threat is not credible and the effect would be limited even if carried out, it does not offer China deterrence options, whether in the diplomatic, military, or economic realms, and this would remain true both in peacetime and in scenarios of crisis or war.[37]

Bilateral Foreign Direct Investment Flows

The level of foreign direct investment (FDI) flows between China and the United States are relatively small given the large volume of trade between the two countries.[38] Many analysts contend that an expansion of bilateral FDI could greatly expand commercial ties.

The U.S. Bureau of Economic Affairs (BEA) reports data on FDI flows to and from the United States.[39] It estimates the cumulative level of Chinese FDI in the United States through the end of 2011 at $3.8 billion on a historical-cost (or book value) basis (see Table 8). In 2011, Chinese FDI flows to the United States were $576 million, a 49.3% drop from the previous year. However, these data do not reflect FDI that Chinese investors may have made through offshore locations (such as Hong Kong) to invest in the United States.[40] Some analysts contend that the BEA's data on China's FDI in the United States do not fully capture all investments. For example, the Rhodium Group (a private research consultancy and advisory company) estimates cumulative Chinese FDI flows to the United States through the end of 2011 at $16.4 billion, and that the amount of new Chinese FDI to the United States in 2011 was $4.5 billion.[41]

U.S. FDI in China is significantly higher than China's FDI in the United States, according to BEA data.[42] Cumulative U.S. FDI in China through 2011 was $54.2 billion.

U.S. FDI flows to China fell by about $8.5 billion in 2009, due largely to the effects of the global economic slowdown. They grew by $7.1 billion in 2010 but fell by $1.7 billion in 2011. BEA estimates that U.S. majority-owned non-bank affiliates in China employed 774,000 workers in China in 2008.[43]

Table 8. U.S. Data on Annual U.S.–China Bilateral FDI Flows: 2005-2011 and Cumulative Value of FDI at Year-End 2011 ($ millions)

	2005	2006	2007	2008	2009	2010	2011	Cumulative: Value of FDI at 2011 Year-End
China's FDI in the United States	146	315	8	500	500	1,169	576	3,815
U.S. FDI in China	1,955	4,226	5,243	15,971	-8,526	7,089	-1,663	54,234

Source: U.S. Bureau of Economic Analysis.

Notes: Cumulative data are on a historical-cost basis. Excludes Chinese FDI in the United States that may have been made through other countries.

Chinese Companies in the United States

Although the level of Chinese FDI in the United States is relatively small, many Chinese firms view the United States as a key part of their efforts to become more globally competitive companies, move closer to their U.S. customers, circumvent perceived trade and investment barriers (such as the Buy American Act), and to avoid U.S. trade remedy measures (such as antidumping duties).

Some examples of Chinese FDI in the United States include the following:

The Dalian Wanda Group Corporation Ltd. on May 21, 2011, announced that it had signed a merger and acquisition agreement to acquire AMC Entertainment (the world's second-largest theater chain) for $2.6 billion.

Suntech Power Holdings Co., Ltd., the world's largest producer of solar panels, opened a solar plant in Goodyear, AZ, in October 2010, employing 100 workers.

Sany Group, a global producer of construction equipment, founded Sany America Inc. in 2006, headquartered in Peachtree City, GA. In 2007, it announced it would invest $100 million to create and establish a manufacturing facility for constructing and engineering Sany products, with expected employment of 300 workers by the time the project is completed.[44]

Wanxiang Group, an automotive parts manufacturer, established Wanxiang America Corporation in 1994, based in Illinois. Over the past decade, Wangxing America reportedly has purchased or invested in more than 20 U.S. firms and employs 5,000 U.S. workers—more than any other Chinese company.[45]

Pacific Centuries Motor (now a subsidiary of AVIC Automobile Industry Co., Ltd, a state-owned firm) purchased Nexteer Automotive, a Michigan-based firm that producers steering and driveline systems, for an estimated $450 million.[46]

Tianjin Pipe Corporation, China's largest steel pipe-maker, announced in 2009 that it planned to spend $1 billion to construct a mini-mill facility in Gregory, TX, that will manufacture steel products from recycled scrap steel. Over the first 10 years of operation, the project is projected to boost the local economy by $2.7 billion and generate $327 million in direct employee salaries.[47]

Haier Group, a major global appliance and electronics firm, maintains its corporate headquarters for Haier America in New York City, has sales offices in 13 U.S. states, and operates a $40 million refrigerator plant in Camden, SC, reportedly the first U.S. manufacturing facility built by a Chinese firm (2000).

ZTE Corporation, one of China's largest telecommunications manufacturers, established a U.S. presence in 1995. ZTE USA is headquartered in Dallas, TX, and maintains R&D facilities in five U.S. states.

Huawei Technologies is a leading global information and communications technology solutions provider. Since gaining a U.S. presence in 2011, Huawei has reportedly partnered with 280 U.S. technology providers, with total procurement contracts exceeding $30 billion, covering such items as software, components, chipsets, and services. In February, Huawei announced procurement contracts with U.S. firms worth $6 billion.[48]

Golden Dragon Precise Copper Tube Group Inc., (one of the world's largest precise copper tube manufacturers) announced in February 2012 that it planned to build a $100 million manufacturing facility in Alabama.

In addition to China's FDI in the United States and its holdings in U.S. Treasury securities, China (as of June 2011) held $159 billion in U.S. equities (such as stocks), up from $3 billion in June 2005. It also held $241 billion in U.S. agency securities, many of which are asset-backed (such as Fannie Mae and Freddie Mac securities),[49] and $16 billion in corporate bonds. The China Investment Corporation (CIC), a sovereign wealth fund established by the Chinese government in 2007 with $200 billion in registered capital to help better manage China's foreign exchange reserves, has been one of the largest Chinese purchasers of U.S. equities and other U.S. assets; it has stakes in such firms as Morgan Stanley, the Blackstone Group, and J.C. Flowers & Co.[50] It appears that many of the investments by the CIC and other Chinese entities have attempted to avoid political controversy in the United States by limiting its ownership shares to less than 10%.

Issues Raised by Chinese FDI in the United States

Many U.S. analysts contend that greater Chinese FDI in the United States, especially in "greenfield" projects (new ventures) that manufacture products or provide services in the United States and create new jobs for U.S. workers,[51] could help improve bilateral economic relations and might lessen perceptions among some critics in the United States that growing U.S.-China trade undermines U.S. employment and harms U.S. economic interests.[52] A number of analysts note that China's outward FDI has been growing rapidly since 2004 and is likely to continue in the years ahead.[53] Such analysts contend that greater efforts should be made by U.S. policymakers to encourage Chinese firms to invest in the United States rather than block them for political reasons. In June 2011, President Obama issued an executive order establishing the "SelectUSA Initiative" to coordinate federal efforts to promote and retain investment in the United States. According to a White House factsheet issued during the U.S. visit of Chinese Vice President Xi Jinping in February 2012, China was already one of SelectUSA top 10 focus markets and that the Administration was planning a significant expansion of the initiative, including with resources dedicated to attracting Chinese investors and facilitating their investment. The two sides further pledged to deepen cooperation on infrastructure financing.[54]

Some critics of China's current FDI policies and practices contend that they are largely focused on mergers and acquisitions that are geared toward boosting the competitive position of Chinese firms and enterprises favored by the Chinese government for development (some of which also may be receiving government subsidies). Some argued that such investments are often made largely to obtain technology and know-how for Chinese firms, but do little to boost the U.S. economy by, for example building new factories and hiring workers. Another major issue relating to Chinese FDI in the United States is the relative lack of transparency of Chinese firms, especially in terms of their connections to the central government. When Chinese state-owned enterprises (SOEs) attempt to purchase U.S. company assets, some U.S. analysts ask what role government officials in Beijing played in that decision. Many U.S. policymakers are troubled by the possibility that efforts by Chinese SOEs to acquire U.S. company assets could be part of a Chinese government's strategy to develop global Chinese firms that may one day threaten the economic viability of U.S. firms at home and abroad. Chinese officials contend that investment decisions by Chinese companies, including SOEs and publicly-held firms (where the government is the largest shareholder), are solely based on commercial considerations, and have criticized U.S. investment policies as "protectionist."

According to the Foreign Investment and National Security Act (FINSA) of 2007 (P.L. 110-149), the Committee on Foreign Investment in the United States (CFIUS) may conduct an investigation on the effect of an investment transaction on national security if the covered transaction is a foreign government-controlled transaction (in addition to if the transaction threatens to impair national security, or results in the control of a critical piece of U.S. infrastructure by a foreign person).[55] The House report on the bill (H.Rept. 110-24, H.R. 556) noted: "The Committee believes that acquisitions by certain government-owned companies do create heightened national security concerns, particularly where government-owned companies make decisions for inherently governmental—as opposed to commercial—reasons."

There have been several instances in which efforts by Chinese firms (oftentimes these have been SOEs or state-favored firms) have raised concerns of some U.S. policymakers and/or U.S. stakeholders:

- In 2004, Lenovo Group Limited, a computer company primarily owned by the Chinese government, signed an agreement with IBM Corporation to purchase IBM's personal computer division for $1.75 billion. Some U.S. officials raised national security concerns over potential espionage activities that could occur in the United States at IBM research facilities by Lenovo employees if the deal went through. A review of the agreement by CFIUS took place in which

IBM and Lenovo were able to address certain national security concerns and, as a result, the acquisition was completed in April 2005.[56]

- In 2005, the China National Offshore Oil Corporation (CNOOC), a Chinese SOE, made a bid to buy UNOCAL, a U.S. energy company, for $18.5 billion, but widespread opposition in Congress led CNOOC to withdraw its bid. Some Members argued at the time that the proposed takeover represented a clear threat to the energy and national security of the United States, would put vital oil assets in the Gulf of Mexico and Alaska into the hands of a Chinese state-controlled company, could transfer a host of highly advanced technologies to China, and that CNOOC's bid to take over UNOCAL would be heavily subsidized by the Chinese government. Some Members argued that "vital" U.S. energy assets should never sold to the Chinese government. CNOOC officials referred to U.S. political opposition to the sale as "regrettable and unjustified."[57]
- In September 2007, Huawei announced plans, along with its partner, Bain Capital Partners, to buy the U.S. firm 3Com Corporation, a provider of data networking equipment, for $2.2 billion. However, the proposed merger was withdrawn in February 2008 following a review of the deal by CFIUS when Huawei and its partner failed to adequately address U.S. national security concerns raised by CFIUS members.[58]
- In July 2009, China's Northwest Nonferrous International Investment Company, a Chinese SOE, made a $26 million offer to purchase a 51% stake in the Firstgold Corporation, a U.S. exploration-stage company. However, the deal reportedly raised national concerns within CFUIS because some of the mines controlled by Firstgold were near U.S. military installations. As a result, the Chinese firm withdrew its bid in December 2009.[59]
- In February 2010, Emcore Corporatation, a provider of compound semiconductor-based components, subsystems, and systems for the fiber optics and solar power markets, announced it had agreed to sell 60% interest in its fiber optics business (excluding its satellite communications and specialty photonics fiber optics businesses) to China's Tangshan Caofeidian Investment Corporation (TCIC) for $27.8 million. However, Emcore announced in June 2010 that the deal had been ended because of concerns by CFIUS.[60]

- In May 2010, Anshan Iron and Steel Group Corporation (Ansteel), a major Chinese state-owned steel producer, announced plans to form a joint venture with Steel Development Company, a U.S. firm in Mississippi, to build and operate four mills to produce reinforcing bar and other bar products used in infrastructure applications, and one mill that would be capable of producing electrical and silicon grades of steel used in energy applications.[61] In July 2010, the Congressional Steel Caucus sent a letter signed by 50 Members to Secretary of the Treasury Tim Geithner, expressing concerns over the effect the investment would have "on American jobs and our national security."[62] At a February 2012 hearing on China's SOEs, Representative Visclosky, chairman of the Congressional Steel Caucus stated: "As a Caucus, we were concerned that the investment would allow a Chinese state-owned enterprise to pursue the government of China's aims, and not the aims of the employer, the American worker, or the market. We were concerned that this investment would allow the full force and financing of the Chinese government to exploit the American steel market from American soil. We also were concerned that China would have access to new steel production technologies and information regarding American national security infrastructure projects."[63]
- In May 2010, Huawei bought certain intellectual property assets of 3Leaf Systems (an insolvent U.S. technology firm) for $2 million. A February 2011 letter issued by Senators Jim Webb and Jon Kyl to Commerce Secretary Gary Locke and Treasury Secretary Tim Geithner stated: "We are convinced that any attempt Huawei makes to expand its presence in the U.S. or acquire U.S. companies warrants thorough scrutiny. Moreover, the 3Leaf acquisition appears certain to generate transfer to China by Huawei of advanced U.S. computing technology. Allowing Huawei and, by extension, communist China to have access to this core technology could pose a serious risk as U.S. computer networks come to further rely on and integrate this technology."[64] In February 2011, Huawei stated that it been formally notified by CFIUS that it should withdraw its application to acquire 3Leaf's assets, which it later did.[65] In an "Open Letter," Huawei invited the U.S. government to carry out a formal investigation on any concerns it may have about Huawei.[66]
- On May 9, 2012, the Federal Reserve announced that it had approved (1) the application by Industrial and Commercial Bank of China

Limited, China Investment Corporation, and Central Huijin Investment Ltd., to become bank holding companies by acquiring up to 80% of the voting shares of the Bank of East Asia (USA) National Association; (2) the Bank of China's application to establish a branch in Chicago, IL; and (3) the application by the Agricultural Bank of China Limited to establish a state-licensed branch in New York City.[67] In a letter to Federal Reserve Chairman Ben Bernanke, Senator Robert Casey noted that each of entities approved by the Federal Reserve was state-owned, and he expressed concern that "these banks and their U.S. subsidiaries will use their state-support as a way to underprice U.S. banks that abide by U.S. law and do not have the support of a sovereign country behind them."[68]

- On September 28, 2012, President Obama issued an executive order requiring Ralls Corporation, a Chinese-owned firm, to divest its interest in four wind farm project companies in Oregon that it acquired earlier in the year, due to national security concerns, reportedly because of their proximity to a naval test facility.[69] China's government-controlled media called the action "protectionist."

Chinese Restrictions on U.S. FDI in China

U.S. trade officials have urged China to liberalize its FDI regime in order to boost U.S. business opportunities in, and expand U.S. exports to China. Although China is one of the world's top recipients of FDI, the Chinese central government imposes numerous restrictions on the level and of types of FDI allowed in China. To a great extent, China's investment policies appear to be linked to industrial policies that seek to promote the development of sectors identified by the government as critical to future economic development. For example, since the early 1980s, the Chinese government has encouraged foreign auto companies to invest in China, but has limited FDI in that sector to 50-50 joint ventures with domestic Chinese partners.[70] In addition, the central government maintains a "Guideline Catalogue for Foreign Investment" (the latest revision was issued in January 2012), which lists FDI categories that are encouraged, restricted, or prohibited.[71] Many of the sectors under the "encouraged" category include high technology, green technology, and energy conservation, and pollution control.[72] Several of the sectors under the "restricted" category limit FDI to joint ventures (such as for rare earth smelting) or where the Chinese parties are the controlling shareholders (such as railway passenger transport companies). "Prohibited" sectors are those that fall under "national security" concerns (such as manufacturing of ammunition and weapons) or are categories where the government seeks to preserve state monopolies (such as postal companies) or protect Chinese firms from foreign competition (such as mining of rare earth elements).

The Chinese government also sets restrictions on FDI inflows during the investment screening process, or through its mergers and acquisition regulations, especially when seeking to protect pillar or strategic industries that the central government (as well as many provincial and local governments) seeks to promote. Many critics of China's investment policies contend that the Chinese government often requires foreign firms to transfer technology to their China partners, and sometimes to set up research and development facilities in China, in exchange for access to China's markets.[73] Foreign-invested firms in China face a number of challenges, including local protectionism, lack of regulatory transparency, IPR theft, and discriminatory license practices.

The United States and China have held negotiations on reaching a bilateral investment treaty (BIT) with the goal of expanding bilateral investment opportunities. U.S. negotiators hope such a treaty would improve the investment climate for U.S. firms in China by enhancing legal protections and dispute resolution procedures, and by obtaining a commitment from the Chinese government that it would treat U.S. investors no less favorably than Chinese investors. However, some groups have argued that a BIT with China could hurt U.S. workers by encouraging more U.S. firms to relocate to China.[74]

In April 2012, the Obama Administration released a "Model Bilateral Investment Treaty" that was developed to enhance U.S. objectives in the negotiation of new BITs.[75] The new BIT model establishes mechanisms to promote greater transparency, labor and environment requirements, disciplines to prevent parties from imposing domestic technology requirements, and measures to boost the ability of investors to participate in the development of standards and technical regulations on a nondiscriminatory basis.

MAJOR U.S.-CHINA TRADE ISSUES

China's economic reforms and rapid economic growth, along with the effects of globalization, have caused the economies of the United States and China to become increasingly integrated.[76] Although growing U.S.-China economic ties are considered by most analysts to be mutually beneficial overall, tensions have risen over a number of Chinese economic and trade policies that many U.S. critics charge are protectionist, economically distortive, and damaging to U.S. economic interests. A 2012 survey by the American Chamber of Commerce in China (AmCham China) of its members in China illustrates the complex nature of the bilateral trade relationship. The survey found that 76% of respondents said that they made a profit in China in 2011, and 86% said they would boost investment in their Chinese operations in 2012. However, 37% of respondents stated that it has become more difficult to obtain business licenses in recent years and 51% said license requirements put them at a competitive disadvantage vis-a-vis domestic Chinese firms.[77] According to the USTR, most U.S. trade disputes with China stem from the consequences of its incomplete transition to a free market economy. Major areas of concern for U.S. stakeholders include

- China's web of industrial policies that seek to promote and protect domestic sectors and firms, especially SOEs, deemed by the government to be critical to the country's future economic growth;
- its failure to provide adequate protection of U.S. intellectual property rights (IPR);
- its mixed record on implementing its obligations in the World Trade Organization (WTO) and its failure to join the WTO's Government Procurement Agreement (GPA); and
- its managed currency policy in which the government intervenes to limit the appreciation of the renminbi (RMB) against the dollar and other major currencies in order to make China's export industries more globally competitive.

Chinese "State Capitalism"

Currently, a significant share of China's economy is thought to be driven by market forces. According to a 2010 WTO report, the private sector now accounts for more than 60% of China's gross domestic product (GDP).[78] However, the Chinese government continues to play a major role in economic decision-making. For example, at the macroeconomic level, the Chinese government maintains policies that induce households to save a high level of their income, much of which is deposited in state-controlled Chinese banks. This enables the government to provide low-cost financing to Chinese firms, especially SOEs. At the microeconomic level, the Chinese government (at the central and local government level) seeks to promote the development of industries that are deemed critical to the country's future economic development by using various policies, such as subsidies, tax breaks, preferential loans, trade barriers, FDI restrictions, discriminatory regulations and standards, export restrictions on raw materials (such as rare earths) technology transfer requirements imposed on foreign firms, public procurement rules that give preferences to domestic firms, and weak enforcement of IPR laws.

Many analysts contend that the Chinese government's intervention in various sectors through industrial policies has intensified in recent years. The December 2011 U.S. Trade Representative's (USTR's) report on China's WTO trade compliance states that since 2006 there has been a "troubling trend in China toward intensified state intervention" and that China seems to be "embracing state capitalism more strongly."[79]

China's Plan to Modernize the Economy and Promote Indigenous Innovation

Many of the industrial policies that China has implemented or formulated since 2006 appear to stem largely from a comprehensive document issued by China's State Council (the highest executive organ of state power) in 1996 titled the *National Medium-and Long-Term Program for Science and Technology Development (2006-2020)*, often referred to as the MLP. The MLP appears to represent an ambitious plan to modernize the structure of China's economy by transforming it from a global center of low-tech manufacturing to a major center of innovation (by the year 2020) and a global innovation leader by 2050.[80] It also seeks to sharply reduce the country's dependence on foreign technology. The MLP includes the stated goals of "indigenous innovation, leapfrogging in priority fields, enabling development, and leading the future."[81] Some of the broad goals of the MLP state that by 2020:

- The progress of science and technology will contribute 60% or above to China's development.
- The country's reliance on foreign technology will decline to 30% or below (from an estimated current level of 50%).
- Gross expenditures for research and development (R&D) would rise to 2.5% of gross domestic product (from 1.3% in 2005). Priority areas for increased R&D include space programs, aerospace development and manufacturing, renewable energy, computer science, and life sciences.[82]

The document states that “China must place the strengthening of indigenous innovative capability at the core of economic restructuring, growth model change, and national competitiveness enhancement. Building an innovation-oriented country is therefore a major strategic choice for China’s future development.” This goal, according to the document, is to be achieved by formulating and implementing regulations in the country’s government procurement law to “encourage and protect indigenous innovation,” establishing a coordination mechanism for government procurement of indigenous innovative products, requiring a first-buy policy for major domestically made high-tech equipment and products that possess proprietary intellectual property rights, providing policy support to enterprises in procuring domestic high-tech equipment, and developing “relevant technology standards” through government procurement.

Reaction by U.S. Stakeholders

Beginning in 2009, several U.S. companies began to raise concerns over a number of Chinese government circulars that would establish an “Indigenous Innovation Product Accreditation” system. For example, in November 2009, the Chinese government released a “Circular on Launching the 2009 National Indigenous Innovation Product Accreditation Work,” requiring companies to file applications by December 2009 for their products to be considered for accreditation as “indigenous innovation products.” U.S. business representatives expressed deep concern over the circulars, arguing that they were protectionist in nature because they extended preferential treatment for Chinese government procurement to domestic Chinese firms that developed and owned intellectual property (IP) and thus largely excluded foreign firms.[83] AmCham China described China’s attempt to link IP ownership with market access as “unprecedented worldwide.”[84] A letter written by the U.S. Chamber of Commerce and 33 business associations to the Chinese government on December 10, 2009, stated that the indigenous innovations circulars would “make it virtually impossible for any non-Chinese companies to participate in China’s government procurement market—even those that have made substantial and long-term investments in China, employ Chinese citizens, and pay taxes to the Chinese government.”[85] Such groups contend that a large share of their technology is developed globally and thus it would be difficult to attribute the share of technology developed in China needed to obtain accreditation.[86]

A 2011 AmCham China survey found that 40% of respondents believed that China’s indigenous innovation policies would hurt their businesses and

26% said their businesses were already being hurt by such policies.[87] At a November 2011 WTO review of China's IPR policies, the U.S. WTO representative stated that China's policies of adopting indigenous innovation had "created a troubling trend toward increased discriminatory policies which were aimed at coercing technology transfer." He stated that "Chinese regulations, rules and other regulatory measures frequently called for technology transfer, and in certain cases, conditioned, or proposed to condition, the eligibility for government benefits or preferences on intellectual property being owned or developed in China, or being licensed, in some cases exclusively, to a Chinese party."[88]

China's Response to U.S. Concerns

The Chinese government responded to U.S. concerns over its indigenous innovation policies by arguing that they did not discriminate against foreign firms or violate global trade rules.[89] However, during the visit of Chinese President Hu Jianto to the United States in January 2011, the Chinese government stated that it would not link its innovation policies to the provision of government procurement preferences.[90] During the May 2011 session of the U.S.-China Strategic and Economic Dialogue (S&ED), China pledged that it would eliminate all of its indigenous innovation products catalogs.[91] During the November 2011 talks held under the U.S.-China Joint Commission on Commerce and Trade (JCCT), the Chinese government announced that the State Council had issued a measure requiring governments of provinces, municipalities, and autonomous regions to eliminate by December 1, 2011, any catalogues or other measures linking innovation policies to government procurement preferences.[92] This occurred after foreign business groups raised concerns that discriminatory indigenous innovation policies might continue to be implemented at the local level even after Hu Jintao's commitment.[93]

Remaining U.S. Concerns

While many U.S. business leaders have applauded China's pledge to delink indigenous innovation from government procurement, some remain wary that China will implement new policies that attempt to provide preferences to local Chinese firms over foreign firms. According to Adam Segal with the Council of Foreign Relations: "Even if China reverses certain policies under U.S. pressure, it will remain dedicated to those goals. U.S. policy is likely to become a game of Whac-a-Mole, beating down one Chinese initiative on indigenous innovation only to see another pop up."[94] U.S. business groups are also concerned with how the MLP blueprint will affect

China's commitment to enforcing foreign IPR. They note, for example, that the MLP states: "Indigenous innovation refers to enhancing original innovation, integrated innovation, and re-innovation based on assimilation and absorption of imported technology, in order to improve our national innovation capability." To some, this seems to indicate that China intends to take existing technology, make some changes and improvements on it, and then claim it as its own without acknowledging or compensating the original IPR holders. A 2011 report by the U.S. Chamber of Commerce stated that China's indigenous innovation policies led many international technology companies to conclude that the MLP is a "blueprint for technology theft on a scale the world has never seen before."[95]

U.S. officials have attempted to convince Beijing that, while its desire to increase innovation in China is a commendable goal, its efforts to limit the participation of foreign firms in such efforts, or attempting to condition market access in China to the development of IPR by foreign firms in China will hinder, not promote, the advancement of innovation in China. The direction China takes on this issue could have a significant impact on U.S. economic interests as noted by a study by the U.S. International Trade Commission (USITC):

> To the extent that China's policies succeed in accelerating technological progress, productivity, and innovation in the Chinese economy, they could provide spillover benefits for other countries. But if indigenous innovation policies act as a form of technological import substitution, systematically favoring Chinese domestic firms over foreign firms in relevant industries, they would be expected to have a negative effect on foreign firms and economies roughly analogous to what would occur if China simply imposed a protective tariff on imports of goods in the relevant sectors or levied a discriminatory excise tax on the sales of FIEs in the Chinese market.[96]

Intellectual Property Rights (IPR)

U.S. business and government representatives have voiced growing concern over economic losses suffered by U.S. firms as a result of IPR infringement in China (and elsewhere), including those that have resulted from cyber attacks. U.S. innovation and the intellectual property that is generated by such activities have been cited by various economists as a critical source of U.S. economic growth and global competitiveness.[97] For example, according to the Department of Commerce, in 2010, U.S. IP-intensive industries supported at least 40 million jobs and contributed $5.1 trillion (or 34.8%) to U.S. gross domestic product (GDP). A study by NDP Consulting estimated that in 2008, workers in IP-intensive production earned 60% more than workers at similar levels in non-IP industries.[98] A study on the Apple iPod concluded that Apple's innovation in developing and engineering the iPod and its ability to source most of its production to low-cost countries, such as China, have helped enable it to become a highly competitive and profitable firm as well as a creator of high-paying jobs (such as engineers engaged in the design of Apple products) in the United States.[99]

Lack of effective and consistent protection of IPR has been cited by U.S. firms as one of the most significant problems they face in doing business in China. Other U.S. firms have expressed concern over pressures they often face from Chinese government entities to share technology and IPR with a Chinese partner. Although China has significantly improved its IPR protection regime over the past few years, U.S. IP industries complain that piracy rates in China continue to remain unacceptably high and economic losses are significant, as illustrated by studies and estimates made by several stakeholders:

- A 2012 AmCham China survey found that 79% of respondents in 2012 felt that China's IPR enforcement was ineffective.[100]
- The USITC estimated that U.S. intellectual property-intensive firms that conducted business in China lost $48.2 billion in sales, royalties, and license fees in 2009 because of IPR violations in China. It also estimated that an effective IPR enforcement regime in China that was comparable to U.S. levels, could increase employment by IP-intensive firms in the United States by 923,000 jobs[101]
- The Business Software Alliance (BSA) estimates the commercial value of illegally used software in China at $7.8 billion in 2010 and that the software piracy rate in China was 78%.[102]
- The U.S. Customs and Border Protection reported that China accounted for 62% of pirated goods seized by the agency in FY2011 (based on domestic value).[103] The value of seized goods originating from China was $110 million.[104]

Chinese officials contend that they have significantly improved their IPR protection regime, but argue that the country lacks the resources and a sophisticated legal system to effectively deal with IPR violations. They also contend that IPR infringement is a serious problem for domestic Chinese firms as well. However, some analysts contend that China's relatively poor record on IPR enforcement can be partially explained by the fact that Chinese leaders want to make China a major producer of capital-intensive and high-technology products, and thus, they are tolerant of IPR piracy if it helps Chinese firms become more technologically advanced. According to an official at the U.S. Chamber of Commerce:

> The newer and emerging challenge to U.S. IPR is not a function of China's lack of political will to crackdown on infringers. Rather, it is a manifestation of a coherent, and government-directed, or at least government-motivated, strategy to lessen China's perceived reliance on foreign innovations and IP. China is actively working to create a legal environment that enables it to intervene in the market for IP, help its own companies to "re-innovate" competing IPR as a substitute to American and other foreign technologies, and potentially misappropriate U.S. and other foreign IP as components of its industrial policies and internal market regulation.... The common themes throughout these policies are: 1) undermine and displace foreign IP; 2) leverage China's large domestic market to development national champions and promote its own IP, displacing foreign competitors in China; and 3) building on China's domestic successes by displacing competitors in foreign markets.[105]

A recent illustration of alleged IPR theft in China involves American Superconductor Corporation (AMSC). On September 14, 2011, AMSC announced that it was filing criminal and civil complaints in China against Sinovel Wind Group Co. Ltd. (Sinovel), China's largest wind turbine producer, and other parties, alleging the illegal use of AMSC's intellectual property. According to an AMSC press release, Sinovel illegally obtained and used AMSC's wind turbine control software code to upgrade its 1.5 megawatt wind turbines in the field to meet proposed Chinese grid codes and to potentially allow for the use of core electrical components from other manufacturers.[106] In addition, AMSC claimed that Sinovel had refused to pay for past shipments from AMSC and was now refusing to honor contracts for future shipments of components and spare parts as well.[107] According to a specialist in intellectual property at Tufts University, "Chinese companies, once they acquire the needed technology, will often abandon their Western partners on the pretext the technology or product failed to meet Chinese governmental regulations. This is yet another example of a Chinese industrial policy aimed at procuring, by virtually any means, technology in order to provide Chinese domestic industries with a competitive advantage."[108]

During the December 2010 U.S.-China Joint Commission on Commerce and Trade (JCCT),[109] the Chinese government announced several new initiatives to improve its IPR protection regime, including boosting purchases of legitimate software by government agencies and 30 large SOEs. The USTR's 2011 Special 301 report noted that China had launched the "Program for Special Campaign on Combating IPR Infringement and Manufacture and Sales of Counterfeiting and Shoddy Commodities" (Special Campaign) in October 2010, aimed at a broad range of IPR violations. The Special Campaign involved 26 member agencies (led by a Chinese vice premier), and reportedly led to improved government coordination of IPR enforcement by the Chinese government.

The USTR's 2012 Special 301 report stated that, while China had made some notable improvements to its IPR enforcement regime (in particular by making the Special Campaign on IPR enforcement permanent), serious problems remain. These include very high levels of trademark counterfeiting and copyright piracy, the persistence of "notorious" physical and online markets selling IPR-infringing goods, the manufacturing and sale of counterfeit pharmaceuticals, export of counterfeit goods, and discriminatory policies seeking to promote indigenous innovation in China by coercing foreign firms to transfer IPR to Chinese domestic firms. The USTR further noted a "recent alarming increase" in thefts of trade secrets (both in China and outside China) for the benefit of Chinese entities. Many of these problems, according to the USTR, stemmed from the lack of an effective government deterrent to such activities. In addition, while China's campaign to require central and provincial governments to use legitimate software produced a "modest increase" in U.S. software to the Chinese government, piracy rates by Chinese SOEs remained high.[110]

Market access in China remains a significant problem for many U.S. IP industries (such as music and films) and is considered to be a significant cause of high IPR piracy rates. For example, until recently, China limited imports of foreign films to 20 per year. During the visit to the United States by Chinese Vice President Xi Jinping (February 13-17, 2012), China agreed that it would allow more American exports to China of 3D, IMAX, and similar enhanced format movies on favorable commercial terms; strengthen the opportunities to distribute films through private enterprises rather than the state film monopoly; and ensure fairer compensation levels for U.S. blockbuster films distributed by Chinese SOEs.[111]

In the 112th Congress, H.R. 3375 (Steve King) would direct the President to impose duties on imports from China equivalent to the estimated annual loss of revenue to U.S. IPR holders resulted from IPR infringement in China. (The United States has challenged China's IPR policies in the WTO, which are discussed later in the report.)

Technology Transfer Issues

When China entered the WTO in 2011, it agreed that foreign firms would not be pressured by government entities to transfer technology to a Chinese partner as part of the cost of doing business in China. However, many U.S. firms argue that this is a common Chinese practice, although this is difficult to quantify because, oftentimes, U.S. business representatives appear to try to avoid negative publicity regarding the difficulties they encounter doing business in China out of concern over retaliation by the Chinese government.[112]

In 2011, U.S. Treasury Secretary Timothy Geithner charged that "we're seeing China continue to be very, very aggressive in a strategy they started several decades ago, which goes like this: you want to sell to our country, we want you to come produce here. If you want to come produce here, you need to transfer your technology to us."[113] The 2012 survey by AmCham China reported that 33% of its respondents stated that technology transfer requirements were negatively affecting their businesses.[114] A 2010 study by the U.S. Chamber of Commerce stated that growing pressure on foreign firms to share technology in exchange for market access in China was forcing such firms to "anguish over balancing today's profits with tomorrow's survival."[115]

However, a 2011 survey by the U.S.-China Business Council found that technology transfer requirements by Chinese entities (both government and private) did not rank among the top 10 challenges faced by the Council's members in 2010. Among U.S. firms where technology was an issue, when asked if their company had been asked to transfer technology to China over the past three years, 18% answered yes. Among the respondents that had been asked to transfer technology, 20% said the pressure came from a government entity, while 80% said that it came from a Chinese company.[116] Of the respondents who said they were asked to transfer technology, 40% stated that they found the requests acceptable, 30% refused the requests, 15% negotiated to mitigate the amount of technology transfer, and 10% said they had to transfer the technology requested in order to gain access to the Chinese market.[117] As noted by the U.S.-China Business Council, China

> has a long-term strategy to bring in foreign technology. But technology is not simply "given to China." Instead, technology is

typically licensed to a China-based entity in which the foreign company has an ownership stake. In many cases the foreign company owns 100 percent of the entity in China; in some cases, the foreign company must form a joint venture with a Chinese partner. In exchange, the company determines a value of the technology to be transferred and negotiates a payment--the technology is rarely "given" for free.[118]

Press reports indicate that the USTR's office is currently seeking information from U.S. manufacturers on examples of efforts by the Chinese government to force the transfer of technology from U.S. companies operating in China. This issue was discussed during President Obama's meeting with Chinese Vice President Xi Jinping on February 14, 2012.[119] A White House Factsheet of the meeting stated: "China reiterates that technology transfer and technological cooperation shall be decided by businesses independently and will not be used by the Chinese government as a pre-condition for market access."

In the 112th Congress, S. 2063 (Webb) would prohibit the transfer by a U.S. commercial entity of any proprietary technology or intellectual property that was researched, developed, or commercialized using a contract, grant, loan, loan guarantee, or other financial assistance provided or awarded by the U.S. government to certain foreign entities (such as those that are owned or controlled by a foreign government) unless the Secretary of Commerce determined (and issued a waiver) that the transfer would not compromise the U.S. economic interests or competitiveness.

Cyber Security Issues

Cyber attacks against U.S. firms have raised concerns over the potential large-scale theft of U.S. IPR and its economic implications for the United States. A 2011 report by McAfee stated that its investigation had identified targeted intrusions into more than 70 global companies and warned that "every conceivable industry with significant size and valuable intellectual property has been compromised (or will be shortly), with the great majority of the victims rarely discovering the intrusion or its impact."[120] Many U.S. analysts and policymakers contend that the Chinese government is a major source of cyber-economic espionage against U.S. firms. For example, Representative Mike Rogers, chairman of the House Permanent Select Committee on Intelligence, stated at an October 4, 2011, hearing that

> attributing this espionage isn't easy, but talk to any private sector cyber analyst, and they will tell you there is little doubt that this is a

> massive campaign being conducted by the Chinese government. I don't believe that there is a precedent in history for such a massive and sustained intelligence effort by a government to blatantly steal commercial data and intellectual property. China's economic espionage has reached an intolerable level and I believe that the United States and our allies in Europe and Asia have an obligation to confront Beijing and demand that they put a stop to this piracy.[121]

According to a report by the U.S. Office of the Director of National Intelligence (DNI): "Chinese actors are the world's most active and persistent perpetrators of economic espionage. U.S. private sector firms and cyber security specialists have reported an onslaught of computer network intrusions that have originated in China, but the IC (Intelligence Community) cannot confirm who was responsible." The report goes on to warn that

> China will continue to be driven by its longstanding policy of "catching up fast and surpassing" Western powers. The growing interrelationships between Chinese and U.S. companies—such as the employment of Chinese-national technical experts at U.S. facilities and the off-shoring of U.S. production and R&D to facilities in China—will offer Chinese government agencies and businesses increasing opportunities to collect sensitive US economic information.[122]

China's Obligations in the World Trade Organization

Negotiations for China's accession to the General Agreement on Tariffs and Trade (GATT) and its successor organization, the WTO, began in 1986 and took over 15 years to complete. During the WTO negotiations, Chinese officials insisted that China was a developing country and should be allowed to enter under fairly lenient terms.

The United States insisted that China could enter the WTO only if it substantially liberalized its trade regime. In the end, a compromise was reached that required China to make immediate and extensive reductions in various trade and investment barriers, while allowing it to maintain some level of protection (or a transitional period of protection) for certain sensitive sectors.

China's WTO membership was formally approved at the WTO Ministerial Conference in Doha, Qatar, on November 10, 2001. On November 11, 2001, China notified the WTO that it had formally ratified the WTO agreements, and on December 11, 2001, it formally joined the WTO.[123]

Under the WTO accession agreement, China agreed to

- reduce the average tariff for industrial goods from 17% to 8.9%, and average tariffs on U.S. priority agricultural products from 31% to 14%;
- limit subsidies for agricultural production to 8.5% of the value of farm output, eliminate export subsidies on agricultural exports, and notify the WTO of all government subsidies on a regular basis;
- within three years of accession, grant full trade and distribution rights to foreign enterprises (with some exceptions, such as for certain agricultural products, minerals, and fuels);
- provide non-discriminatory treatment to all WTO members, such as treating foreign firms in China no less favorably than Chinese firms for trade purposes;
- end discriminatory trade policies against foreign invested firms in China, such as domestic content rules and technology transfer requirements;
- implement the WTO's Trade-Related Aspects of Intellectual Property Rights (TRIPS) Agreement upon accession (which sets basic standards on IPR protection and rules for enforcement);
- fully open the banking system to foreign financial institutions within five years (by the end of 2006); and
- allow joint ventures in insurance and telecommunication (with various degrees of foreign ownership allowed);

WTO Implementation Issues

Getting China into the WTO under a comprehensive trade liberalization agreement was a major U.S. trade objective during the late 1990s. Many U.S. policymakers at the time maintained that China's WTO membership would encourage the Chinese government to deepen market reforms, promote the rule of law, reduce the government's role in the economy, further integrate China into the world economy, and enable the United States to use the WTO's dispute resolution mechanism to address major trade issues. As a result, it was hoped, China would become a more reliable and stable U.S. trading partner. U.S. trade officials contend that in the first years after it joined the WTO, China made noteworthy progress in adopting economic reforms that facilitated its transition toward a market economy and increased its openness to trade and

FDI. However, beginning in 2006, progress toward further market liberalization appeared to slow. By 2008, U.S. government and business officials noted evidence of trends toward a more restrictive trade regime.[124] The USTR's 10th annual report to China on WTO compliance (issued in December 2011) identified several areas of concern, including[125]

- failure by the Chinese government to maintain an effective IPR enforcement regime (discussed below);
- industrial policies and national standards that attempt to promote Chinese firms (while discriminating against foreign firms);
- restrictions on trading and distribution rights;
- discriminatory and unpredictable health and safety rules on imports (especially agricultural products); and
- burdensome regulations and restrictions on services, and failure to provide adequate transparency of trade laws and regulations.

As of November 2012, the United States has brought 14 dispute settlement cases against China, nine of which have been resolved or ruled upon.[126] China has brought six WTO cases against the United States as well.[127] The U.S. cases are summarized below.

Pending U.S. Cases against China

- On September 17, 2012, the USTR announced that it had initiated a WTO dispute settlement casc against China over it export subsidies to auto and auto parts manufacturers in China.[128]
- On May 2012, the United States initiated a WTO dispute settlement case China's improper use of anti-dumping and countervailing duties on broiler products.
- On March 13, 2012, the United States, Japan, and the European Union jointly initiated a dispute settlement case against China's restrictive export policies (such as quotas, tariffs, and minimum export prices) on rare earths and two other minerals.[129]

Resolved Cases or a WTO Panel Has Issued a Ruling[130]

- On September 15, 2010, the USTR's office announced it was bringing a WTO case against China over its improper application of antidumping duties and countervailing duties on imports of grain oriented flat-rolled electrical steel from the United States. A WTO panel in June 2012 ruled largely in favor of the U.S. position and this was generally upheld by a WTO Appellate Body in October 2012.

- On September 15, 2010, the USTR's office announced it was bringing a WTO dispute settlement case against China over its discrimination against U.S. suppliers of electronic payment services (EPS). The United States charged that China permits only a Chinese entity (China UnionPay) to supply electronic payment services for payment card transactions denominated and paid in RMB in China, that service suppliers of other Members can only supply these services for payment card transactions paid in foreign currency, that China requires all payment card processing devices to be compatible with that entity's system and that payment cards must bear that company's logo, and that the Chinese entity has guaranteed access to all merchants in China that accept payment cards, while services suppliers of other WTO members must negotiate for access to merchants.[131] On July 16, 2012, the USTR announced that the United States had largely prevailed in the dispute
- On June 23, 2009, the United States brought a case against China's export restrictions (such as export quotas and taxes) on raw materials (bauxite, coke, fluorspar, magnesium, manganese, silicon metal, silicon carbide, yellow phosphorus, and zinc). The United States charges that such policies are intended to lower prices for Chinese firms (steel, aluminum, and chemical sectors) in order to help them obtain an unfair competitive advantage. China claims that these restraints are intended to conserve the environment and exhaustible natural resources. In July 2011, a WTO panel issued a report that China's export taxes and quotas on raw materials violated its WTO commitments. It further found that China failed to show that restrictions were linked to conservation of exhaustible natural resources for some of the raw materials or to protect the health of its citizens (by reducing pollution).[132] China appealed the WTO panel's ruling. However, on January 30, 2012, a WTO Appellate Body affirmed that China's export quotas and export taxes on certain raw materials violated its WTO commitments.[133] U.S. Trade Representative Ron Kirk called the decision a "tremendous victory for the United States," and said that it would ensure that "core manufacturing industries in this country can get the materials they need to produce and compete on a level playing field."[134]

- On December 22, 2010, the USTR's office announced that it would bring a WTO case against China over a government program that extended subsidies to Chinese wind power equipment manufacturers that use parts and components made in China rather than foreign-made parts and components. On June 7, 2011, the USTR's office announced that China had agreed to end these subsidies. However, the USTR noted that it had taken significant investigatory efforts by the U.S. government, working with industry and workers, to uncover China's wind subsidies because of the lack of transparency in China. The USTR further noted that, under the terms of China's WTO accession, it was required to fully report its subsidy programs to the WTO, which, to date, it has failed to do.[135]
- On December 19, 2008, the USTR filed a WTO case against China over its support for "Famous Chinese" brand programs, charging that such programs utilize various export subsidies (including cash grant rewards, preferential loans, research and development funding to develop new products, and payments to lower the cost of export credit insurance) at the central and local government level to promote the recognition and sale of Chinese brand products overseas. On December 18, 2009, the USTR announced that China had agreed to eliminate these programs.
- On March 3, 2008, the USTR requested WTO dispute resolution consultations with China regarding its discriminatory treatment of U.S. suppliers of financial information services in China. On November 13, 2008, the USTR announced that China had agreed to eliminate discriminatory restrictions on how U.S. and other foreign suppliers of financial information services do business in China.
- On April 10, 2007, the USTR filed a WTO case against China, charging that it failed to comply with the TRIPS agreement (namely in terms of its enforcement of IPR laws). On January 26, 2009, the WTO ruled that many of China's IPR enforcement policies failed to fulfill its WTO obligations. On June 29, 2009, China announced that it would implement the WTO ruling by March 2010.
- On April 10, 2007, the USTR filed a WTO case against China charging that it failed to provide sufficient market access to IPR-related products, namely in terms of trading rights and distribution services. In August 2009, a WTO panel ruled that many of China's regulations on trading rights and distribution of films for theatrical release, DVDs, music, and books and journals were inconsistent with

China's WTO obligation. China appealed the decision, but lost, and in February 2010 stated that it would implement the WTO's ruling.

- On February 5, 2007, the USTR announced it had requested WTO dispute consultations with China over government regulations that give illegal (WTOinconsistent) import and export subsidies to various industries in China (such as steel, wood, and paper) that distort trade and discriminate against imports.[136] China's WTO accession agreement required it to immediately eliminate such subsidies. On November 29, 2007, China formally agreed to eliminate the subsidies in question by January 1, 2008.
- On March 30, 2006, the USTR initiated a WTO case against China over its use of discriminatory regulations on imported auto parts, which often applied the high tariff rate on finished autos (25%) to certain auto parts (which generally average 10%). The USTR charged that that the purpose of China's policy was to discourage domestic producers from using imported parts and to encourage foreign firms to move production to China. On February 13, 2008, a WTO panel ruled that China's discriminatory tariff policy was inconsistent with its WTO obligations (stating that the auto tariffs constituted an internal charge rather than ordinary customs duties, which violated WTO rules on national treatment). China appealed the decision, but a WTO Appellate Body largely upheld the WTO panel's decision.
- On March 18, 2004, the USTR announced it had filed a WTO dispute resolution case against China over its discriminatory tax treatment of imported semiconductors. The United States claimed that China applied a 17% value-added tax (VAT) on semiconductor chips that were designed and made outside China, but gave VAT rebates to domestic producers. Following consultations with the Chinese government, the USTR announced on July 8, 2004, that China agreed to end its preferential tax policy by April 2005. However, the USTR has expressed concern over new forms of financial assistance given by the Chinese government to its domestic semiconductor industry.

During his State of the Union Address in January 2012, President Obama announced plans to create a new Trade Enforcement Unit "charged with investigating unfair trade practices in countries like China." On February 28, 2012, President Obama issued an executive order establishing the Interagency Trade Enforcement Center within the USTR's office. Many analysts contend that the new enforcement unit could result in a sharp increase in the number of WTO dispute settlement cases brought by the United States against China.

China's Accession to the WTO Government Procurement Agreement (GPA)

Government procurement policies are largely exempt from WTO rules, except for those members which have signed the GPA.[137] When China joined the WTO, it indicated its intention to become a member of WTO's GPA as soon as possible, but, to date, has failed to submit an offer acceptable to current GPA members.

China's accession to the GPA is a major U.S. priority. Chinese annual public procurement spending is estimated to range from $88 billion to $200 billion.[138] However, China has established a number of restrictive government procurement practices and policies that favor domestic Chinese firms. Because of China's rapidly growing economy and significant infrastructure needs, China's accession to the GPA could result in significant new opportunities for U.S. firms China did not formally enter into negotiations to join the GPA until 2007, and its initial offer was deemed unacceptable by the other WTO GPA parties. China promised to revise its GPA offer, but did not do so until July 2010. That offer was deemed an improvement over the previous offer but was not accepted, in part because it excluded purchases by local and provincial governments as well as SOEs. A revised offer in December 2011 only covered public entities in three cities and two provinces.[139] Commenting on China's last offer, the USTR's office stated:

> China began its negotiations to join the GPA four years ago this month. Since that time, China has submitted three offers, each an improvement over the last. But China still has some distance to go before the procurement that it is offering is comparable to the extensive procurement that the United States and other Parties cover under the GPA. For example, we are urging China to cover state-owned enterprises, add more sub-central entities and services, reduce its thresholds for the size of covered contracts, and remove other broad exclusions.[140]

Congressional concerns over China's restrictions on public procurement and failure to date to join the GPA have resulted in the introduction of legislation in 112th Congress. H.R. 375 (Kildee) would limit the total value of Chinese goods that could be procured by the U.S. government to the same value of U.S. goods procured by the Chinese government in the previous year, while H.R. 2271 (Royce) would prohibit the federal government from awarding contracts to Chinese entities until China signs the GPA. China reportedly pledged that it would submit a new offer by December 5, 2012.[141]

China's Currency Policy[142]

Unlike most advanced economies (such as the United States), China does not maintain a market-based floating exchange rate. Between 1994 and July 2005, China pegged its currency, the renminbi (RMB) or yuan, to the U.S. dollar at about 8.28 yuan to the dollar.[143] In July 2005, China appreciated the RMB to the dollar by 2.1% and moved to a "managed float," based on a basket of major foreign currencies, including the U.S. dollar. In order to maintain a target rate of exchange with the dollar (and other currencies), the Chinese government has maintained restrictions and controls over capital transactions and has made large-scale purchases of U.S. dollars (and dollar assets).[144] According to the Bank of China, from July 2005 to July 2009, the dollar-yuan exchange rate went from 8.27 to 6.83 yuan per dollar, an appreciation of 21.1%.[145] However, once the effects of the global financial crisis became apparent, the Chinese government halted its appreciation of the RMB and subsequently kept the yuan/dollar exchange rate relatively constant at 6.83 from July 2009 to June 2010 in order to help limit the impact of the sharp decline in global demand for Chinese products.

Many U.S. policymakers, labor groups, and business representatives of import-sensitive industries have charged that, despite minor reforms, the Chinese government continues to actively intervene in currency markets to keep the value of the RMB artificially low against the dollar. They claim that this policy provides an indirect subsidy to Chinese exporters (which makes Chinese goods less expensive in the United States), while acting as a de facto tariff on U.S. goods imported into China (which makes them more expensive). They argue that this policy has particularly hurt several U.S. manufacturing sectors that are forced to compete against low-cost Chinese products and has led to significant job losses in the United States, especially in manufacturing. Critics further charge that China's currency policy has been a major factor in the size and growth of the U.S. trade deficit with China. Some Members of Congress contend that, given the current high rate of unemployment in the United States, Chinese "currency manipulation" can no longer be tolerated.

Chinese officials have insisted that the current currency policy is not meant to favor exports over imports, but instead to foster domestic economic stability.[146] They have expressed concern that abandoning the currency policy, especially given the current state of the global economy, could further weaken its export industries and cause wide-scale layoffs of Chinese workers. Chinese officials view economic stability as critical to sustaining political stability. They further note that China's global trade surplus has declined sharply over the past few years. On June 19, 2010, the Chinese central bank, the People's Bank of China (PBC) stated that, based on current economic conditions, it had decided to "proceed further with reform of the RMB exchange rate regime and to enhance the RMB exchange rate flexibility." From June 2010 to May 2012, the RMB rose by 13% in real (inflation-adjusted) terms against the dollar, and by 40% in real terms overall since currency reform began in 2005. China's current account surplus as a percent of GDP (a figure some analysts use to indicate the level of the yuan's undervaluation) has fallen significantly in recent years, from a historical high of 10.1% in 2007 to 2.8% in 2011, and is projected by the International Monetary Fund (IMF) to decline to 2.3% for 2012.[147] U.S. officials have urged China to continue to liberalize its currency regime and to rebalance the economy by boosting consumer demand (which would increase import demand) and decreasing the reliance on exports and fixed investment for economic growth.

According to the Department of the Treasury, the RMB appreciated by 9.3% against the dollar from June 2010 through November 9, 2012, and by 12.6% on a real (inflation-adjusted) basis. Since 2005, the RMB has appreciated by 40% in real terms.[148] However, some U.S. officials complain that China's exchange rate with the dollar has changed little in 2012. To illustrate, the yuan/dollar exchange rate on January 1, 2012, was 6.30, while on November 13, 2012, it was 6.29, an appreciation of about 0.2%.

Numerous bills have been introduced in Congress over the past few years that would seek to induce China to reform its currency policy or would attempt to address the perceived effects that policy has on the U.S. economy. For example, one bill in the 108th Congress would have imposed an additional duty of 27.5% on imported Chinese products unless China appreciated its currency to near market levels. In the 111th Congress, the House passed an amended version of H.R. 2378 (Tim Ryan), which would have made certain misaligned currencies (such as the RMB) actionable under U.S. countervailing duty cases on foreign government export subsidies (although the Senate did not take up the bill).

The bill was re-introduced in the 112th Congress in the House and Senate (see H.R. 639 and S. 328, discussed below).

Currency Legislation in the 112th Congress

- S. 1619 (Sherrod Brown) which passed the Senate on October 11, 2011, by a vote of 63 to 35, would provide for the identification of fundamentally misaligned currencies and require action to correct the misalignment for certain "priority" countries. The bill would require the Treasury Department to issue a semiannual report to Congress on international monetary policy and currency exchange rates, determine which major global currencies are in fundamental misalignment, and designate certain misaligned currencies for priority action. Treasury would be required to seek negotiations with countries designated for priority action. If efforts were not made to correct the currency misalignment, the following actions would be taken in regard to that country: (1) The Commerce Department would be required to factor in the estimated level of currency undervaluation when determining antidumping duties; (2) the President would be required to prohibit the procurement by the federal government of products or services from the country unless it is a party to the WTO's GPA; (3) the Overseas Private Investment Corporation (OPIC) would not be able to approve any new financing (including insurance, reinsurance, or guarantee) with respect to a project located within the country;[149] (4) the U.S. Executive Director at each multilateral bank would be told to oppose the approval of any new financing to the government of a country, or for a project located within a country, that issues a currency designated for priority action. If a country that has a currency designated for priority action failed to take steps to eliminate the fundamental misalignment within 360 days after its designation by the Treasury Department, the following would occur: (1) the USTR would be required to initiate a dispute resolution case against the priority country, and (2) the Treasury Department would be required to consult with the Federal Reserve System to consider undertaking remedial intervention in international currency markets. The bill would also amend U.S. countervailing duty law to require the Commerce Department to initiate an investigation to determine whether currency undervaluation is providing, directly or indirectly, a countervailing subsidy and makes clarifications to U.S. countervailing law similar to provisions in H.R. 639 and S. 328.
- H.R. 639 (Sander Levin) and S. 328 (Sherrod Brown) would make a "fundamentally undervalued currency" an actionable subsidy under

U.S. countervailing duty law (dealing with government export subsidies).[150] The bills would seek to clarify that a fundamentally undervalued currency could be treated by the Department of Commerce as a benefit conferred by a foreign government to its exports.[151] In addition, the bill seeks to clarify that, in the case of a subsidy relating to a fundamentally undervalued currency, the fact that the subsidy (i.e., the undervalued currency) may have also benefitted non-exporting firms (in addition to exporting firms), would not, for that reason alone, mean that the subsidy could not be considered to be a measure that is contingent upon export performance. The bill directs the Commerce Department to use, if possible, data and methodologies utilized by the IMF to estimate the real effective exchange rate undervaluation of the currency for the purposes of assessing countervailing duties.[152] Factors used to determine a fundamentally undervalued currency would include (over an 18-month period): protracted and large-scale intervention in currency markets; a real effective exchange rate estimated to be undervalued by at least 5%; and foreign asset reserves held by the government that are (1) greater than the amount needed to repay its debt obligations over the next year, (2) 20% of the nation's money supply, and (3) the value of the country's imports over the previous four months.

- S. 1130 and S. 1267 (both by Rockefeller) would, among other things, treat "exchange rate manipulation" as an actionable subsidy under U.S. countervailing duty cases. Exchange rate manipulation would be defined as protracted large-scale intervention by a country to undervalue the country's currency in the exchange market that prevents effective balance-of-payments adjustment or that gains an unfair competitive advantage over any other country.
- S. 1238 (Olympia Snowe) would require that, before Congress approves any bill implementing a free trade agreement or extending permanent normal trade relations status to another country, the President would have to first certify that the government of the potential trading partner has not, in the 10 years preceding the certification, manipulated its currency for the purposes of gaining an unfair advantage in international trade.

Some Members has expressed opposition to various currency bills, arguing that they violate U.S. obligations in the WTO. Other Members have argued that while inducing China to adopt a market-based exchange rate is an important goal, the United States should give higher priority to addressing China's industrial policies and IPR infringement, which some view as more damaging to U.S. economic interests.

THE U.S.-CHINA STRATEGIC AND ECONOMIC DIALOGUE

On September 29, 2006, President George W. Bush and Chinese President Hu Jintao agreed to establish a Strategic Economic Dialogue (SED) to have discussions on major economic issues at the "highest official level." According to a U.S. Treasury Department press release, the intent of the SED was to "discuss long-term strategic challenges, rather than seeking immediate solutions to the issues of the day," in order to provide a stronger foundation for pursuing concrete results through existing bilateral economic dialogues.[153] The first meeting was held in December 2006. Four subsequent rounds of talks were held (the last was in December 2008).

While attending the G-20 summit in London on the global financial crisis on April 1, 2009, President Obama and Chinese President Hu agreed to continue the high-level forum, renaming it the U.S.-China Strategic and Economic Dialogue (S&ED). The new dialogue is based on two tracks. The first (the "Strategic Track") is headed by the Secretary of State on the U.S. side and focuses on political and strategic issues, while the second track (the "Economic Track") is headed by the U.S. Treasury Secretary on the U.S. side and focuses on financial and economic issues. Areas of discussion include economic and trade issues, counterterrorism, law enforcement, science and technology, education, culture, health, energy, the environment (including climate change), non-proliferation, and human rights.

One of the reported benefits of the S&ED process is that it brings together top economic officials from both sides, as well as U.S. Cabinet officials and Chinese heads of ministries, on a regular basis, which enables both sides to identify their major positions and priorities on various issues and to develop long-term working relationships. Some in Congress have criticized the S&ED forum, arguing that it produces few concrete results, and that many of the results described in subsequent fact sheets that are jointly issued simply re-state agreements or pledges China has already made. Others counter that U.S. engagement with China occurs on multiple levels throughout the year and that the S&ED meetings are in part a cumulative result of this process.

The July 2009 Economic Track Session

The first round of the S&ED was held in Washington, DC, on July 27-28, 2009, and involved 12 U.S. Cabinet officials and agency heads and 15 Chinese ministers, vice ministers, and agency heads. The session was focused heavily on issues relating to the global economic crisis. Secretary of the Treasury Timothy Geithner stated: "Recognizing that cooperation between China and the United States will remain vital not only to the well-being of our two nations but also the health of the global economy, we agreed to undertake policies to bring about sustainable, balanced global growth once economic recovery is firmly in place."

The two sides agreed to establish a framework of cooperation based on four pillars:

- Advancing macroeconomic and structural policies to achieve sustainable and balanced growth;
- Promoting more resilient, open, and market-oriented financial systems;
- Strengthening trade and investment ties; and
- Strengthening the international financial architecture.

These pillars appear to have been aimed at deepening bilateral cooperation in response to the global economic crisis, continuing commitments on both sides to promote policies that seek to achieve more balanced economic growth, encouraging China to continue economic and financial reforms, expanding China's role and/or participation in international economic forums,[154] and attempting to avoid new forms of trade protection.

May 2010 Economic Track Session

The May 24-25, 2010, S&ED economic session focused heavily on the continuing efforts relating to the four pillars identified in the July 2009 session. Although few concrete accomplishments were announced at the end of the meetings, the two agreed to intensify talks on a number of bilateral economic and trade issues. The two sides pledged to

- Sign a cooperation protocol on small and medium-sized firms (SMEs);

- Boost economic cooperation at the central and local government level, such as promoting the establishment of state-to-province and city-to-city partnerships;
- Conduct "intensive expert and high-level discussions" as early as the summer of 2010 on innovation issues (such as China's indigenous innovation proposals) and to take into account the results of these talks in formulating and implementing their innovation measures;[155]
- Improve cooperation to address health and safety issues relating to U.S. sales of soybeans to China;
- Establish a cooperative mechanism between the U.S. Export-Import Bank and the Export-Import Bank of China on trade finance, and to develop initiatives to promote exports by SMEs;
- Explore the possibility of cooperating to enable the United States to treat China as a market economy, and to treat certain Chinese firms as market-oriented industries, for the purpose of U.S. trade remedy laws; and
- Boost investment opportunities and transparency.[156]

The May 2011 Economic Track

The third round of the S&ED was held in Washington, DC, on May 9-10, 2011. Prior to the meeting, U.S. officials identified several goals for the economic track of the S&ED, including ensuring that China followed through on previous economic and trade commitments (such as on IPR protection and indigenous innovation policies) and encouraging China to make a number of reforms to its financial sector (such as adopting market-based interest rates on bank deposits and expanding market access in China for U.S. financial firms). China pledged to continue to promote domestic consumption, improve IPR enforcement, eliminate all of its indigenous innovation products catalogues, improve transparency of its economic and trade policies, and provide significant new opportunities for U.S. financial services firms in China.

The May 2012 Economic Track

The fourth S&ED round was held in Beijing on May 3 and 4, 2012, and focused largely on economic rebalancing and boosting foreign access to China's financial services sector.[157] China pledged that it would:

- Increase the number of SOEs that pay dividends;
- Participate in negotiations (beginning in the summer of 2012) for new rules on official export financing with the United States and other major exporters;
- Provide non-discriminatory treatment to all enterprises, regardless of type of ownership, in terms of credit, taxation, and regulatory policies so that U.S. firms can more easily compete against Chinese SOEs;
- Submit a new robust offer in 2012 to join the WTO's GPA and to intensify efforts to negotiate a BIT with the United States;
- Open up more sectors to FDI and improve the transparency of its investment approval process;
- Prioritize the protection of trade secrets, extend efforts to promote the use of legal software by Chinese enterprises, treat IPR owned or developed in other countries the same as IPR owned or developed in China, and hold discussions with U.S. officials on the implementation of China's commitment not to make technology transfer a pre-condition for doing business in China;
- Take steps to raise household income and lower prices of consumer goods, such as cutting import tariffs, reducing taxes on services, and raising deposit rates; and
- Expand market access to domestic financial markets by boosting the permitted level of foreign investment in its stock and bond markets, raising the permitted foreign equity stake in domestic securities joint ventures from 33% to 49%, and allowing foreign investors to establish joint venture brokerages to trade commodity and financial futures (with up to a 49% equity stake).

CONCLUSION

China's rapid economic growth and emergence as a major economic power have given China's leadership increased confidence in its economic model. The key challenges for the United States are to convince China that (1) it has a stake in maintaining the international trading system, which is largely responsible for its economic rise, and to take a more active leadership role in maintaining that system; and (2) further economic and trade reforms are the surest way for China to expand and modernize its economy. For example, by boosting domestic spending and allowing its currency to appreciate, China would likely import more, which would help speed economic recovery in other countries, promote more stable and balanced economic growth in China, and lessen trade protectionist pressures around the world. Improving IPR protection in China and providing non-discriminatory treatment to foreign IP firms would likely foster greater innovation in China and attract more FDI in high technology than has occurred under current policies. Lowering trade barriers on imports would increase competition in China, lower costs for consumers, and boost economic efficiency. Some observers contend that reformist-minded officials in China will continue to push for greater free-market reforms, while others argue that vested interests in China (such as SOEs and export-oriented firms) who benefit from the status-quo will make further economic reforms more difficult to realize.

Opinions differ as to the most effective way of dealing with China on major economic issues:

- Some support a policy of high-level engagement with China using various forums, such as the U.S.-China S&ED, in order to try to resolve complex and long-term issues and prevent either side from imposing new protectionist measures.
- Others support a somewhat mixed policy of using engagement with China when possible, coupled with greater use of WTO dispute settlement procedures to address China's unfair trade policies. Some Members contend that the S&ED forum has failed to produce many tangible results and have advocated using the S&ED to induce China to agree to measurable targets or goals for reducing trade and investment barriers and improving IPR measures that can be used in future meetings to determine China's progress.
- Still others, who see China's economic policies as damaging to U.S. economic interests, advocate a more aggressive U.S. trade policy towards China that uses all available tools available to U.S. policies, including multilateral institutions (such as the WTO and International Monetary Fund), as well as U.S. trade remedy laws (such as antidumping and countervailing measures) to counter the negative effects of China's "unfair trade practices."[158] Some Members have argued that the United States should insist on trade and investment reciprocity with China to ensure a more "balanced" economic relationship.

End Notes

[1] For more information on China's economy, see CRS Report RL33534, *China's Economic Conditions*, by Wayne M. Morrison. For general information on U.S.-China political ties, see CRS Report R41108, *U.S.-China Relations: Policy Issues*, by Susan V. Lawrence and David MacDonald.

[2] The United States suspended China's MFN status in 1951, which cut off most bilateral trade. China's MFN status was conditionally restored in 1980 under the provisions set forth under Title IV of the 1974 Trade Act, as amended (including the Jackson-Vanik freedom-of-emigration provisions). China's MFN status (which was re-designated under U.S. trade law as normal trade relations status, or NTR) was renewed on an annual basis until January 2002, when permanent NTR was extended to China (after it joined the WTO in December 2001).

[3] U.S.-China Business Council, *Testimony on China's WTO Compliance*, September 17, 2012.

[4] U.S. trade data for 2012 are estimates based on actual data for January-September 2012.

[5] This was a slowdown from 2010 when U.S. exports to China increased by 32.1% over the previous year.

[6] However, China's share of U.S. exports in 2011 was lower than the 7.2% level that occurred in 2010.

[7] As noted earlier, U.S. exports to China rose by 5.8% during the first nine months of 2012 over the same period in 2011. The slowdown in U.S. exports to China appears to be partly the result of China's slowing economy. China's gross domestic product (GDP) growth slowed from 10.4% in 2010 to 9.2% in 2011, and is projected to slow to 7.8% in 2012. China's exports and imports during the first nine months of 2012, grew by 7.7% and 5.0%, respectively over the same period in 2011, which was considerably slower than export and import growth in the same period in 2011over 2010 levels (22.7% and 26.6%, respectively).

[8] China's real GDP growth from 2008 to 2011 averaged 9.6%.

[9] Boston Consulting Group, *Big Prizes in Small Places: China's Rapidly Multiplying Pockets of Growth,* November 2010, p. 10.

[10] *Bloomberg*, "China's Millionaires Jump Past 1 Million on Savings, Expansion of Economy," June 1, 2011.

[11] The Chinese government's ability to fund these projects is enhanced by the fact that its debt levels are much smaller relatively to those of other major economies. For example, China's central government budget deficit as a percent of GDP in 2011 was 1.6% versus 8.7% for the United States. China's public debt as a percent of GDP at the end of 2011 was 16.1% versus 66.1% for the United States. Source: *Economist Intelligence Unit*, Country Data, database.

[12] China Daily, "China Mobile phone users exceed 1 billion," March 20, 2012, at http://www.chinadaily.com.cn/china/2012-03/30/content_14954435.htm.

[13] Boeing Corporation, *Current Market Outlook: 2011-2030*, June 2011.

[14] Internet World Stats, at http://www.internetworldstats.com/stats.htm.

[15] HIS Global Insight, *World Car Industry Forecast Report*, September 2011.

[16] For additional information on the U.S. auto industry in China, see CRS Report R40924, *China's Auto Sector Development and Policies: Issues and Implications*, by Rachel Tang.

[17] USA Today, *GM sells more vehicles in China than in U.S*, January 21, 2011.

[18] According to GM's website, it currently has 11 joint ventures and two wholly owned foreign enterprises in China where it employees more than 35,000 workers.

[19] Pacific Rim countries include Australia, Brunei, Cambodia, China, Hong Kong, Indonesia, Japan, South Korea, Laos, Macao, Malaysia, New Zealand, North Korea, Papua New Guinea, the Philippines, Singapore, Taiwan, Thailand, Vietnam, and several small island nations.

[20] U.S. manufactured imports from Pacific Rim countries minus China as a percent of total U.S. manufactured imports fell from 43.5% in 1990 to 20.8% in 2011.

[21] China's accession to the WTO (with the reduction of trade and investment barriers) appears to have been a major factor behind the migration of computer production from other countries to China.

[22] USITC, *How Much of Chinese Exports Is Really Made In China? Assessing Foreign and Domestic Value-Added in Gross Exports*, report number 2008-03-B, March 2008, p. 21.

[23] Communications of the ACM, *Who Captures Value in a Global Innovation Network? The Case of Apple's iPod*, March 2009.

[24] In comparison, the simple average MFN applied tariff rate for other major emerging markets was as follows: Russia (9.5%), India (13.0%), and Brazil (13.7%).

[25] USTR,*2012 National Trade Estimate of Foreign Trade Barriers*, March 2012, p. 68.

[26] U.S. data on FDI flows to and from China differ from Chinese data on FDI flows to and from the United States. This section examines only U.S. data.

[27] Investment is often a major factor behind trade flows. Firms that invest overseas often import machinery, parts, and other inputs from the parent company to manufacture products for export or sale locally. Other such invested overseas firms may produce inputs and ship them to their parent company for final production.

[28] 15 CFRS 806.15(a)(1). The 10% ownership share is the threshold considered to represent an effective voice or lasting influence in the management of an enterprise. See BEA, *International Economic Accounts, BEA Series Definitions*, available at http://www.bea.gov /international.

[29] BEA also reports FDI data according to broad industrial sections, including mining; utilities; wholesale trade; information; depository institutions; finance (excluding depository institutions); professional, scientific, and technical services; non-bank holding companies; manufacturing (including food, chemicals, primary and fabricated metals, machinery, computers and electronic products, electrical equipment, appliances and components, transportation equipment, and other manufacturing); and other industries.

[30] For additional information on this issue, see CRS Report RL34314, *China's Holdings of U.S. Securities: Implications for the U.S. Economy*, by Wayne M. Morrison and Marc Labonte.

[31] The Treasury Department estimates that China's total holdings of U.S. government and private securities were $1.7 trillion as of June 2011, of which, 76% ($1.3 trillion) were in U.S. Treasury securities.

[32] China's large annual trade surpluses and inflows of FDI are major contributors to China's accumulation of foreign exchange reserves, which totaled $3.2 trillion as of June 2012.

[33] However, over the past years, Chinese officials have expressed concern over the "safety" of their large holdings of U.S. debt. They worry that growing U.S. government debt and expansive monetary policies will eventually spark inflation in the United States, resulting in a sharp depreciation of the dollar. This would diminish the value of China's dollar asset holdings.[33] Some Chinese officials have called for replacing the dollar as the world's major reserve currency with some other currency arrangement, such as through the International Monetary Fund's special drawing rights system, although many economists question whether this would be a feasible alternative in the short run.

[34] Some observers characterize foreign holdings of U.S. Treasury securities as "foreign ownership of U.S. government debt."

[35] China may have sold some of its holdings. In addition, some of China's holdings may have matured and the Chinese government decided not to re-invest the money in new U.S. Treasury securities. The drop in China's holdings of U.S. Treasury securities appears to have caused in part by a slow-down in China's accumulation of foreign exchange reserves. From June 2011 to June 2012, those reserves rose by 1.3%, compared to a 30.5% increase from June 2010 to June 2011.

[36] The bill, titled the National Defense Authorization Act for Fiscal Year 2012, passed the House on May 26, 2011.

[37] Office of the Secretary of Defense, *Report to Congress, Assessment of the National Security Risks Posed to the United States as a Result of the U.S. Federal Debt Owed to China as a Creditor of the U.S. Government*, July 2012.

[38] Note, U.S. and Chinese data on FDI flows between each other differ.

[39] According the BEA, direct investment implies that a person in one country has a lasting interest in, and a degree of influence over the management of, a business enterprise in another. As such, it defines FDI as ownership or control of 10% or more of an enterprise's voting securities, or the equivalent, is considered evidence of such a lasting interest or degree of influence over management.

[40] To reflect this, the BEA attempts to measure the level of FDI inflows according to the country of "ultimate beneficial owner" (UBO). BEA's standard measurement of China's cumulative FDI in the United States was $3.2 billion in 2010 (the most recent year available); using the UBO calculation raised this figure to $5.8 billion (86% higher), indicating a significant amount of Chinese FDI in the United States is through other countries. See BEA UBO tables at http://www.bea.gov/international/di1fdibal.htm.

[41] Rhodium Group, *China Investment Monitor, Tracking Chinese Direct Investment in the U.S.* at http://rhgroup.net/interactive/china-investment-monitor.

[42] According to Chinese data, the United States is a relatively large source of FDI in China, ranking fourth in cumulative FDI through 2011.

[43] BEA, U.S. *Direct Investment Abroad: Financial and Operating Data for U.S. Multinational Companies*, available at http://www.bea.gov/international/di1usdop.htm.

[44] Sany America website at http://www.sanyamerica.com/about-sany-america.php#ribbon.

[4]5 Washington Post, "Job creation seen as key to China's investment in U.S," January 19, 2011,available at http://www.washingtonpost.com/wp-dyn/content/article/2011/01/18 /AR2011011806676.html.

[46] The purchase reportedly represents China's biggest single investment in the global auto parts-making industry and will make the Chinese company the largest private employer in Saginaw, Michigan at nearly 3,000 (Source: New York Times, *G.M. Sells Parts Maker to a Chinese Company,* November 29, 2010). The firm owns 20 manufacturing plants worldwide, 5 regional engineering and test centers, and 14 local customer support centers.

[47] Xinhua News Agency, "U.S official hails Chinese Project in Texas, October 11, 2011."

[48] http://www.prnewswire.com/news-releases/huawei-poised-to-sustain-tens-of-thousands-of-job-opportunities-for-usbusinesses-139525078.html.

[49] U.S. Department of the Treasury, *Preliminary Report on Foreign Portfolio Holdings of U.S. Securities at End-June 2011*, February, 29, 2012.

[50] For more information on the CIC, see CRS Report R41441, *China's Sovereign Wealth Fund: Developments and Policy Implications*, by Michael F. Martin.

[51] According to the BEA, Chinese majority-owned nonbank affiliates in the United States employed 1,700 U.S. workers in 2006 (most recent data available).

[52] During the 1980s, Japanese firms significantly boosted their FDI in the United States, such as in automobile manufacturing, in part to help to alleviate bilateral trade tensions.

[53] China reports that its overseas FDI in 2010 was $68.8 billion, ranking it fifth in the world. China's accumulated overseas FDI through 2010 was $317.2 billion.

[54] The White House, *Joint Fact Sheet on Strengthening U.S.-China Economic Relations*, February 14, 2012.

[55] CFIUS is an interagency committee that serves the President in overseeing the national security implications of foreign investment in the U.S. economy. See CRS Report RL33388, *The Committee on Foreign Investment in the United States (CFIUS)*, by James K. Jackson.

[56] IBM and Lenovo reportedly agreed to address national security concerns by CFIUS. For example, it was agreed that 1,900 employees from a North Carolina research facility, which IBM had shared with other technology companies, would move to another building. See the *Financial Times*, "US State Department limits use of Chinese PCs," May 18, 2006.

[57] The Senate report of its version of FINSA (S.Rept. 110-80, S. 1610) noted that CNOOC's attempt to acquire UNOCAL "led many members of Congress to raise questions about the transfer of ownership or control of certain sectors of the U.S. economy to foreign companies, especially to foreign companies located within or controlled by countries the governments of which might not be sympathetic to U.S. regional security interests."

[58] Although Huawei states that it is a private company wholly owned by its employees, many analysts contend that the company has close connections to the Chinese military. In addition, Huawei has also reportedly received extensive financial support from the Chinese government, including a $30 billion line of credit from China Development Bank.

[59] *New York Times*, "Chinese Withdraw Offer for Nevada Gold Concern," December 21, 2009.

[60] Emcore Press Release, June 28, 2010, available at http://www.emcore.com/news_events/release?y=2010&news=249.

[61] A press release by Ansteel stated that its intensions are "to capitalize on the opportunity to enter into an overseas joint venture with a company that is focused on utilizing advanced technology in an environmentally friendly and highly profitable manner." See, http://www.steeldevelopment.com/documents/ansteel2010.pdf.

[62] See letter at http://visclosky.house.gov/SC_Geithner_CFIUS_7.2.10.pdf.

[63] Testimony of Congressman Peter J. Visclosky before the U.S.-China Economic and Security Review Commission on China's State-Owned and State-Controlled Enterprises, February 15, 2012.

[64] The letter also raised concerns over allegations that Huawei had ties to the Iranian government, had received substantial subsidies from the Chinese government, and had a poor record of protecting intellectual property rights.

[65] Huawei initially stated that it would decline CFIUS's recommendation with the intent of going through all of the procedures of the CFIUS process (including a potential decision by the President) in order to "reveal the truth about Huawei."

[66] Huawei, Open Letter, February 25, 2011, available at http://www.huawei.com/huawei_open_letter.do.

[67] Senator Robert Casey, *Press Release*, May 10, 2012, available at http://www.federalreserve.gov.

[68] The letter is available at http://www.casey.senate.gov/newsroom/press/release/?id=b940fb00-0a69-42d6-bcff6ac72c8ce0c1.

[69] New York Times, *Obama Orders Chinese Company to End Investment at Sites Near Drone Base*, September 28, 2012. Available at http://www.nytimes.com/2012 /09/29/us/politics /chinese-company-ordered-to-give-up-stake-inwind-farms-near-navy-base.html.

[70] The automotive industry was designated a "pillar industry" by the Chinese government in 1991.

[71] China also maintains a permitted category which represents a neutral position by the government that FDI is neither encouraged or discouraged. Prior to 2012, FDI in the manufacture of complete automobiles was listed as an encouraged category.

[72] One major function of the Guideline Catalogue for Foreign Investment is to promote FDI in sectors that the government has targeted for growth in its five-year macro-economic plans.

[73] USTR, 2011 *Report to Congress On China's WTO Compliance*, December 2011, p.7.

[74] *Inside U.S.-China Trade*, April 28, 2010.

[75] The Administration began efforts to review and revise the U.S. BIT model in 2009. The previous BIT model dated to 2004. The Administration's review process likely meant that negotiations with China for a BIT were someone limited.

[76] The impact of globalization has been a controversial topic in the United States. Some argue that it has made it easier for U.S. firms to shift production overseas, resulting in lost jobs in the United States (especially in manufacturing) and lower wages for U.S. workers. Others contend that globalization has induced U.S. firms to become more efficient and to focus a greater share of their domestic manufacturing on higher-end or more technologically advanced production (while sourcing lower-end production abroad), making such firms more globally competitive. The result has been that the United States continues to be a major global manufacturer in terms of value-added, but there are fewer U.S. workers in manufacturing.

[77] AmCham China. 2012 China Business Climate Survey Report, March 2012, available at http://www.amchamchina.org/businessclimate2012.

[78] World Trade Organization, *Trade Policy Review Body, Trade Policy Review, Report by the Secretariat, China*, Revision, 2010, Part 2, p.1.

[79] U.S. Trade Representative, *2011 USTR Report to Congress on China's WTO Compliance,* December 2011, p.2.

[80] As some observers describe it, China wants to go from a model of "made in China" to "innovated in China."

[81] The MLP identifies main areas and priority topics, including energy, water and mineral resources, the environment, agriculture, manufacturing, communications and transport, information industry and modern service industries, population and health, urbanization and urban development, public security, and national defense. The report also identifies 16 major special projects and 8 "pioneer technologies."

[82] *R&D Magazine*, December 22, 2009.

[83] U.S. business representatives also claim that the Chinese government is using tax incentives, standards setting and requirements, security regulations, subsidies, technology transfer requirements, and other measures to promote the goals of indigenous innovation.

[84] AmCham China,*2011 White Paper*, April 26, 2011, p. 66.

[85] A copy of the letter can be found at http://online.wsj.com/public/resources /documents /chinaprocurementletter1210.pdf.

[86] Some U.S. business representatives argue that one of the main goals of China's indigenous innovation regulations is to induce foreign firms to boost their R&D activities in China in order to qualify for government contracts.

[87] However 68% of the respondents stated that they were unaffected by indigenous innovation policies and 6% said they had benefited. See AmCham China, 2011 *China Business Climate Survey.*

[88] Transitional Review Under Section 18 of the Protocol on the Accession of the People's Republic of China, Report to the General Council by the Chair, November 17, 2011, p.4.

[89] Wall Street Journal, *China Defends Rule On 'Indigenous' Tech*, December 15, 2009.

[90] The White House, *U.S. - China Joint Statement*, January 19, 2011.

[91] According to a U.S. fact sheet on the meeting "China pledged to eliminate all of its government procurement indigenous innovation products catalogues and revise Article 9 of the draft Government Procurement Law Implementing Regulations (which have preferences in government procurement to national indigenous innovation products), in fulfillment of President Hu's January 2011 commitment not to link Chinese innovation policies to government procurement preferences. See U.S. Department of the Treasury, The 2011 U.S.-China Strategic and Economic Dialogue U.S. Fact Sheet – Economic Track, May 10, 2011.

[92] U.S. Department of Commerce, *22nd U.S.-China Joint Commission on Commerce and Trade Fact Sheet*, November 21, 2011.

[93] The U.S.-China Business Council reported in February 2011 that it had identified 22 municipal and provincial governments that had issued at least 61 indigenous innovation catalogues. U.S. business representatives sought to ensure that Beijing's pledge on indigenous innovation would apply at all levels of government in China. See U.S.- China Business Council, *Provincial and Local Government Indigenous Innovation Catalogues*, February 2011.

[94] Foreign Affairs, *China's Innovation Wall: Beijing's Push for Homegrown Technology*, September 28, 2010.

[95] U.S. Chamber of Commerce, *China's Drive for 'Indigenous Innovation' - A Web of Industrial Policies*, February 2011, p.4.

[96] USITC, China: Intellectual Property Infringement, Indigenous Innovation Policies, and Frameworks for Measuring the Effects on the U.S. Economy (Investigation No. 332-514, USITC Publication 4199, November 2010, p.6-7.

[97] See CRS Report RL34292, *Intellectual Property Rights and International Trade*, by Shayerah Ilias and Ian F. Fergusson.

[98] Nam Pham, *The Impact of Innovation and the Role of Intellectual Property Rights on U.S. Productivity, Competitiveness, Jobs, Wages and Exports*, 2010, NDP Consulting.

[99] Communications of the ACM, *Who Captures Value in a Global Innovation Network? The Case of Apple's iPod*, March 2009.

[100] AmCham China, *2012 China Business Climate Survey Report*, March 2012, available at http://www.amchamchina.org/businessclimate2012.

[101] The United States International Trade Commission, *China: Effects of Intellectual Property Infringement and Indigenous Innovation Policies on the U.S. Economy*, USITC Publication 4226, May 2011, p. xiv.

[102] BSA, *Eighth Annual Global Software Piracy Study*, May 2011, available at http://portal.bsa.org/globalpiracy2010/downloads/study_pdf/2010_BSA_Piracy_Study-Standard.pdf.

[103] This rate goes up to 80% if seizures of goods from Hong Kong is included.

[104] U.S. Customs and Border Protection, *Intellectual Property Rights, Fiscal Year 2011 Seizure Statistics*, February 2012, available at http://www.cbp.gov/linkhandler /cgov/trade/priority_ trade/ipr/ipr_communications/seizure/ipr_seizures_fy2011.ctt/ipr_ seizure_fy2011.pdf.

[105] Testimony of Jeremie Waterman, Senior Director, Greater China, U.S. Chamber of Commerce, before the U.S. International Trade Commission, *Hearing on China: Intellectual Property Infringement, Indigenous Innovation Policies, and Frameworks for Measuring the Effects on the U.S. Economy*, June 15, 2010.

[106] AMSC claims Sinovel had obtained the intellectual property from a former AMSC employee who was now under arrest in Austria for economic espionage and fraudulent manipulation of data.

[107] AMSC Press Release, "AMSC Filing Criminal and Civil Complaints Against Sinovel," September 14, 2011.

[108] "Data Theft Case May Test U.S. China Ties," *Boston Globe*, September 19, 2011.

[109] The JCCT was established in 1983 to serve as a forum for high-level dialogue on major bilateral trade issues.

[110] USTR, *2012 Special 301 Report*, April 2012, available at http://www.ustr.gov/sites /default/files/2012%20Special%20301%20Report_0.pdf.

[111] The White House, *Press Release*, February 17, 2012, at http://www.whitehouse.gov/the-press-office/2012/02/17/united-states-achieves-breakthrough-movies-dispute-china.

[112] China denies that public officials exert such pressure and that any technology transfers that do occur in China are the result of commercial agreements between companies.

[113] Reuters, September 23, 2011.

[114] AmCham China, *2012 China Business Climate Survey Report*, March 2012, available at http://www.amchamchina.org/businessclimate2012

[115] U.S. Chamber of Commerce, *China's Drive for 'Indigenous Innovation' - A Web of Industrial Policies,* July 29, 2010.

[116] However, the Council notes that since the Chinese government maintains approval authority for investment decisions, which may be used by Chinese firms as leverage when attempting to negotiate technology transfer agreements with U.S. firms.

[117] Ibid.

[118] U.S. China Business Council, *USCBC 2011 China Business Environment Survey Results: Market Growth Continues, Companies Expand, But Full Access Elusive for Many,* November 2011, p.20.

[119] Inside Trade, *USTR Seeks Info From Manufacturers On Forced Technology Transfer To China,* January 31, 2012.

[120] The report did not indentify China (or any country) as the source of the intrusions. McAfee, *Revealed: Operation Shady Rat, An Investigation of Targeted Intrusions Into More Than 70 Global Companies, Governments, and Non-Profit Organizations During the Last Five Years*, 2011.

[121] House Permanent Select Committee on Intelligence, *Chairman Mike Rogers Opening Statement at the Hearing on Cyber Threats and Ongoing Efforts to Protect the Nation,* October 4, 2011.

[122] DNI, Office of the National Counterintelligence Executive, *Foreign Spies Stealing U.S. Economic Secrets in Cyberspace, Report to Congress on Foreign Economic Collection and Industrial Espionage*: 2009-2011, October 2011.

[123] Following China's WTO accession, the United States, in January 2002, granted China permanent normal trade relations (PNTR) status (prior to that time, that status was on a conditional basis) to ensure that the United States and China had a formal trade relationship under the rules of the WTO.

[124] China generally implemented its tariff reductions on schedule.

[125] USTR, *2011 Report to Congress on China's WTO Compliance*, December 2011.

[126] For an overview of the WTO's dispute settlement process, see CRS Report RS20088, *Di Settlement in the World Trade Organization (WTO): An Overview*, by Daniel T. Sl Brandon J. Murrill, and Jane M. Smith.

[127] China has brought five cases against the United States. These have included challenges to applications of antidumping and countervailing measures, restrictions on imports of Chi poultry, and U.S. safeguard measures restricting imports of Chinese tires.

[128] China argued that the "Buy America" provisions of the American Recovery and Reinvestm Act of 2009 and U.S. State government procurement laws conferred a subsidy to U producers.

[129] For additional information on China's restrictions on rare earths, see CRS Report R4251 *China's Rare Earth Industry and Export Regime: Economic and Trade Implications for th United States*, by Wayne M. Morrison and Rachel Tang.

[130] Often, cases are resolved through consultations before a case goes to a panel.

[131] WTO, *Dispute Settlement—Certain Measures Affecting Electronic Payments, Current Status*, August 31, 2012.

[132] A summary of the WTO panel report can be found at http://www.wto.org/english /tratop_e/dispu_e/cases_e/ ds394_e.htm#bkmk394r.

[133] The Appellate Body declared moot and of no legal effect the Panel's findings regarding China's export licensing requirements, minimum export price requirements, administration and allocation of export quotas, and fees and formalities in connection with exportation because of inadequacies in the complainants' panel requests involving these measures.

[134] USTR, *Press Release*, January 31, 2012.

[135] USTR *Press Release*, June 7, 2011, available at http://www.ustr.gov/about-us/press-office/press-releases/2011/june/ china-ends-wind-power-equipment-subsidies-challenged.

[136] Some programs gave tax preferences, tariff exemptions, discounted loans, or other benefits to firms that met certain export performance requirements, while others gave tax breaks for purchasing Chinese-made equipment and accessories over imports.

[137] The GPA is a plurilateral agreement among 41 WTO members (including the United States, Japan, and the 27 members of the European Union) that effectively provides market access for various non-defense government procurement projects to signatories to the agreement. Each member of the Agreement submits lists of government entities and goods and services (with thresholds and limitations) that are open to bidding by firms of the other GPA members. WTO members that are not signatories to the GPA, including those that are GPA observers (such as China), do not enjoy any rights under the GPA. Nor are non-GPA signatories in the WTO generally obligated to provide access to their government procurement markets.

[138] Testimony of Karen Laney, Acting Director of Operations, U.S. International Trade Commission before the Subcommittee on Terrorism, Nonproliferation, and Trade, Committee on Foreign Affairs, on *China's Indigenous Innovation, Trade, and Investment Policies*, March 9, 2011.

[139] Inside U.S. Trade, December 8, 2011.

[140] USTR Press Release, December 2011.

[141] *Inside U.S. Trade's China Trade Extra*, November 13, 2012.

[142] For additional information on this issue, see CRS Report RS21625, *China's Currency Policy: An Analysis of the Economic Issues*, by Wayne M. Morrison and Marc Labonte.

[143] The official name of China's currency is the renminbi, which is denominated in units of yuan.

[144] Much of China's trade is believed to be in U.S. dollars (e.g., exporters are often paid in dollars). The central government requires firms to exchange most of their dollars for RMB.

of China data using the official government "middle rate."

) exchange rate is a relatively common practice among developing ly those that want to attract foreign investment and expand exports. A ge rate, such as one tied to the U.S. dollar, attempts to signal foreign e value of their investments will not be affected by the type of large swings es that can occur under a floating exchange rate regime. Given the current a's economy and trade flows, most economists question whether the of China's currency policy is appropriate.

IF stated that the RMB was "substantially undervalued" against a broad basket s, but in 2012, it changed that designation to "moderately undervalued."

ment of the Treasury, *Report to Congress on International Economic and Rate Policies*, November 27, 2012, p. 13.

sion would not affect China because OPIC is already prohibited by U.S. law from g in China.

lls are identical and are the same legislation passed by the House (H.R. 2378) in nber 2010. The Senate did not take up the bill.

nefit would be defined as the difference between the amount of foreign currency ived by the exporter from the transaction and the amount that would have been received ne currency was not undervalued.

a summary of U.S. trade remedy laws, see CRS Report RL32371, *Trade Remedies: A rimer*, by Vivian C. Jones.

S. Treasury Department press release, December 15, 2006.

he United States is seeking to broaden China's participation in international economic institutions in order to promote the goal of helping to make China a "responsible stakeholder" in the global economy. This implies that, since China greatly benefits from the global trading system and is a major global economy, it should shoulder a greater responsibility in maintaining and promoting that system (rather than just enjoying the benefits of that system

155 The United States also pledged that it would review Chinese concerns relating to U.S. restrictions on high technology exports to China resulting from the current U.S. export control regime.

156 The United States pledged that it welcomed investment from China and confirmed that review of foreign investment by the Committee on Foreign Investment in the United States ensures the consistent and fair treatment of all foreign investment without prejudice to the place of origin. China promised to revise its Catalogue Guiding Foreign Investment in Industries and encourage and expand areas open to foreign investment, including those relating to high-technology, energy, and the environment. China also pledged to streamline the process for investment approval.

157 The session was somewhat overshadowed by events relating to Chinese human rights advocate Chen Guangcheng who had been temporarily sheltered at the U.S. embassy in Beijing prior to the session.

158 On March 13, 2012, President Obama signed into law H.R. 4105 (P.L. 112-99), which clarifies that U.S. countervailing duty law can be applied to subsidized goods from nonmarket economy countries (such as China), and that the Department of Commerce can adjust antidumping duties applied to goods from nonmarket economy countries when countervailing duties are applied to the same goods. The measure was enacted in response to a December 2011 Court of Appeals decision that held that U.S. law prohibits the Department of Commerce from applying countervailing duties to non-market economies

and to comply with a WTO ruling over applying both countervailing and antidumpi measures on imports. See CRS Report RL33976, *U.S. Trade Remedy Laws and Nonmark Economies: A Legal Overview*, by Jane M. Smith.

In: U.S.-China Trade: Issues and Patterns ISBN: 978-1-62618-538-8
Editor: Josephine A. Gonzalez

Chapter 2

PATTERNS IN U.S.-CHINA TRADE SINCE CHINA'S ACCESSION TO THE WORLD TRADE ORGANIZATION*

Joseph Casey

With Supporting Research and Contributions by:
Shelly Zhao, USCC Research Fellow
David Herbert, USCC Research Fellow
Meghan Crossin, USCC Research Fellow
John Dotson, USCC Research Coordinator

EXECUTIVE SUMMARY

Following China's accession to the World Trade Organization (WTO) in December 2001, expectations were high that U.S. exports to China would increase due to reduced tariffs and increased market access. An examination of trade data from 2000 to 2011 demonstrates the following patterns in U.S.-China trade that have taken place in the decade since China's accession to the WTO:

* This report was released by the U.S.-China Economic and Security Review Commission, November 2012.

1. U.S. exports to China have more than quintupled in value but are dwarfed by the surge of Chinese imports into the United States, resulting in a steadily growing bilateral trade deficit;
2. A dramatic rise in the levels of non-manufactured goods (particularly agricultural products, raw materials, and mined natural resource products) exported by U.S. producers to China, to the extent that there is now a U.S. trade surplus with China in non-manufactured goods;
3. A dramatic rise in imports of Chinese-made manufactured goods into the United States, and a significant decrease in U.S. exports of manufactured goods to China as a share of total exports;
4. A steady move up the value chain for Chinese imports into the United States – most noticeably in computers and consumer electronics. However, in this latter category China often serves as an assembly and export platform for multinational corporations of components manufactured elsewhere in world, a fact that may not be clearly reflected in trade statistics.

Key Findings (2011 vs. 2000 Trade Data)

Non-manufactured products accounted for roughly twice as large a share of U.S. exports to China in 2011 as in 2000. In 2000, the United States ran a trade deficit with China in non-manufactured goods. By 2009, this deficit had become a surplus. Points worthy of note include:

- Agricultural exports from the United States to China have increased primarily as a result of increased soybean exports. (Soybeans are primarily used in China as animal feed.) Other major exports like cotton and smaller exports like tobacco have also seen significant growth. There will likely be continued growth in U.S. agricultural exports to China, based both on U.S. productive capacity and on China's large and urbanizing population. Chinese imports of U.S. cast-offs (scrap metal, waste paper, and the like) surged by 916 percent over the 2000-2008 period.[1] China was the largest foreign market for U.S. exports of iron and steel waste and scrap in 2011, with a nearly 28 percent increase from the previous year. From 2005 to 2011, U.S. exports of iron and steel waste and scrap to China increased from $1.6 billion to $2.6 billion.The waste trade is highly reliant upon commodity prices and has been driven by China's rapid development.[2]

- According to the U.S. International Trade Commission's 2011 report, *Shifts in U.S. Merchandise Trade*, China was the single largest source of U.S. imports by value in 2010. The largest increases in U.S. exports to China were agricultural products, motor vehicles and semiconductor manufacturing equipment.[3]
- Exports of oil, gas, minerals and ores from the United States to China also grew substantially over this period: from around $105 million U.S. dollars (USD) in 2000 to $2.1 billion USD in 2010. Exports in this category more than doubled in value from 2009 to 2010 alone. This increase can be primarily attributed to exports of metal ores, and coal and petroleum gases, and has once again likely been driven by China's rapid development.

Concurrently, there was a growing U.S. trade deficit with China in regards to manufactured goods from 2000 to 2011. The key categories of U.S.-made manufactured goods exported to China over this period remained computers and electronics, transportation equipment, chemicals and machinery. Points worthy of note include:

- The largest source of the expanded deficit was increased imports of computers and electronic products from China. While U.S. exports of computer and electronic products to China saw a shift from fully manufactured products to components (such as semi-conductors), there was a concurrent increase in imports of fully manufactured electronics and computers from China.
- The relative share of chemicals exports from 2000 to 2011 remained stable, but an increased proportion by 2011 was resin, rubber and basic chemicals. These exports may be used for infrastructure, packaging, and industrial purposes. There was a significant decline in pesticides, fertilizers and agricultural chemicals. Pharmaceuticals, one of the largest categories of U.S. chemical exports to the world as a whole, make up only a small percentage of U.S. chemical exports to China.
- The relative share of transportation equipment exports also remained relatively stable from 2000 to 2011. The United States continued to export a high amount of aviation equipment, but also exported more cars (especially in the last several years). Both the airplane and car markets may be continued growth sectors.

- While the relative share of U.S. machinery exports to China dropped slightly from 2000 to 2011, machinery exports jumped from around $6.5 billion in 2009 to $10.7 billion in 2011.

Although China still provided high levels of low-value added products like toys and shoes to the United States, computers and electronic products came to make up a larger share of U.S. imports from China in the period from 2000 to 2011.

- Exports other than computers and electronic products from China to the United States still accounted for roughly $1.9 trillion in cumulative export value from 2000-2011, while computers and electronic products, on the other hand, accounted for over $950 billion.
- Domestic trends in China, like inflation, higher wages and an aging population, may decrease China's long-term competitiveness in exporting low-value added products, like toys and shoes. Therefore, higher tech products should come to make up an increasing share of Chinese exports in the future.
- Most of the computers and electronic products exported from China to the United States are still relatively low-tech items, such as notebook computers, telephones, televisions and video games.
- Although trade statistics credit the entire manufacturing value of these computers and electronic products to China, in many cases the value added in China may be little more than assembly. The perceived limited value added by China to these higher tech exports may explain one Chinese motivation for policies like "indigenous innovation" – a desire to essentially transform the meaning of the ever-present label "Made in China" into "Made in China by Chinese Firms".

Introduction – WTO Expectations

When China became the 143rd member of the World Trade Organization (WTO) on December 11, 2001, it "also committed to take concrete steps to remove trade barriers and open its markets to foreign companies and their exports from the first day of accession in virtually every product sector and for a wide range of services."[4]

Perhaps of greatest significance for U.S. exports, under the WTO accession agreement China agreed to reduce the average tariff for industrial goods and agriculture products to 8.9 percent and 15 percent, respectively (with most cuts made by 2004 and all cuts completed by 2010).[5]

Moreover, there were specific restrictions on key agricultural products that China lifted when it entered the WTO,[6] and they agreed to limit subsidies for agricultural production and eliminate subsidies on agricultural exports.

There were expectations that WTO entry would benefit U.S. exports to China because it would open the Chinese market to foreign firms, expand trading rights, and lead to both immediate and delayed tariff reductions. In a press conference on March 29, 2000, President Clinton summed up this optimistic viewpoint:

> The United States doesn't lower any tariffs. We don't change any trade laws. We do nothing. They have to lower tariffs. They open up telecommunications for investment.
>
> They allow us to sell cars made in America in China at much lower tariffs. They allow us to put our own distributorships over there. They allow us to put our own parts over there.
>
> We don't have to transfer technology or do joint manufacturing in China anymore. This is a hundred-to-nothing deal for America when it comes to the economic consequences.[7]

President Clinton also predicted that "this agreement will create jobs for America, it will create jobs for labor union members,"[8] and many others agreed. Perhaps embodying the spirit of the moment, Doug Bandow of the Cato Institute proclaimed that "[t]he silliest argument against [granting China market access in the United States] is that Chinese imports would overwhelm U.S. industry. In fact, American workers are far more productive than their Chinese counterparts."[9]

As a result of this confidence, most of the debate surrounding China's accession to the WTO had little to do with economics[10] and instead focused on issues like human rights, political concerns and the environment.

So what has actually happened since China entered the WTO? How have the expectations of 2001 actually played out over the past decade? And what factors have caused the U.S. trade deficit with China to more than triple between 2000 and 2011?

In order to better understand how patterns in U.S.-China trade have changed over the course of the last decade, this report will compare official

U.S. trade statistics from 2000 (the last full year before China entered the WTO) and 2011.[11]

After a brief overview of the current trade balance, this report will examine exports and imports in particular sectors in greater detail and explicate some of the trends in U.S.-China trade that the statistics reveal.

GROWTH OF EXPORTS, GROWTH OF IMPORTS, GROWTH OF DEFICIT

According to the U.S.-China Business Council (USCBC), China became the 3rd largest U.S. export market in 2007,[12] a ranking it continued to maintain through 2011.[13] U.S. exports to China increased by an average of 18.4 percent from 2000 to 2011, resulting in growth of over 468 percent for the decade.[14] In comparison, U.S. exports to the rest of the world increased by 55 percent.[15] According to the Foreign Trade Division of the U.S. Census Bureau, U.S. total exports to China increased from roughly $16.2[16] billion in 2000 to $91.9 billion in 2010.[17] In 2011, U.S. exports to China totaled $103.9 billion.[18]

The increasing purchasing power of China's 1.3 billion citizens, coupled with China's goals of modernizing its infrastructure, upgrading its industries and improving rural living standards has led many trade analysts to argue that China could become an even more significant market for U.S. exports in the future.[19]

On the othcr hand, in absolute terms imports from China into the United States have outpaced exports from the United States to China since China entered the WTO. China has gone from being the eighth largest source of U.S. imports in 1990 to the fourth in 2000, to the second in 2004-2006, and the first by 2007.[20] China was the largest source of U.S. goods imports in 2011 at $399 billion.[21]

As a result, according to the Foreign Trade Division of the U.S. Census Bureau, the U.S.-China trade balance has ballooned from $83.8 billion in 2000 to $295 billion in 2011. In sum, though U.S. exports to China have grown since 2000, the overall value of exports has been dwarfed by imports from China, resulting in a major trade imbalance.

To better understand the drivers of export growth from the U.S. to China, this report will next examine the changing composition of exports from the U.S. to China during the period from 2000 to 2011.[22]

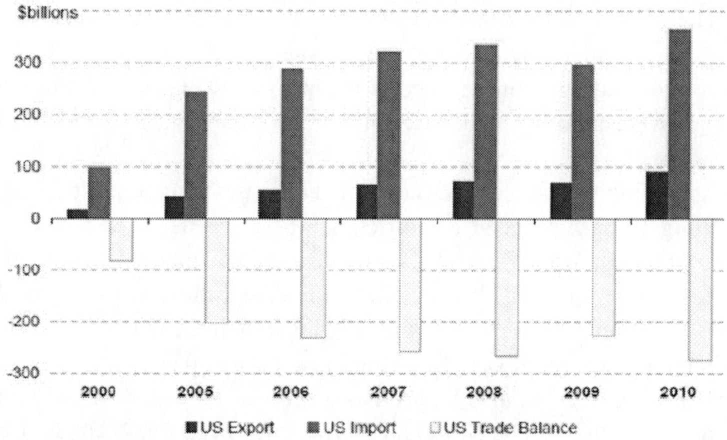

Source: U.S. International Trade Commission DataWeb.

Figure 1. U.S.-China Trade Balance. [23]

Transshipping and Relocated Production

Although this report relies upon officially reported U.S.-China trade statistics, an unknown portion of U.S. exports to and imports from China are transshipped via an intermediary location. The most important transshipping point for China is Hong Kong, due to its lower taxes and freer trade regulations as compared to the rest of China. While it is difficult to distinguish between U.S.-Hong Kong trade and U.S.-China trade transshipped through Hong Kong, the impact of such transshipping upon the U.S.-China trade balance cannot be discounted. A Congressional Research Service report noted that there were two main types of discrepancies caused by differing U.S.-China transshipment calculations:

- The exporting country lists the intermediary as the destination, whereas the importing country lists the exporting country as the origin.
- Shipment via the intermediary country changes the value of the goods when they are en route between origin and destination countries. This issue of value differences reportedly accounts for almost half of the discrepancy between U.S. and Chinese trade statistics.[24]

Transshipment thus leads to different U.S. and Chinese trade balance calculations, with the United States understating U.S. exports to China, and China understating Chinese exports to the United States; and the United States overestimating the overall trade imbalance, while China underestimates it.

According to one team of economic analysts, "adjusting for re-exports via Hong Kong... reduced the difference between the U.S. and Chinese trade deficit for 2005 from $87.4 billion to $26.5 billion."[25] In 2010, the United States reported a trade deficit of $273 billion with China; U.S. exports to China grew by 32 percent, imports from China grew by 23 percent, and the overall U.S.-China deficit grew by 20 percent.[26]

Transshipping can also be used as a measure to evade and undermine anti-dumping duties. The USCC raised this issue in its 2004 Annual Report in analysis of the effect of the impact of China's entry into the WTO upon the U.S. textile and apparel manufacturing industry. As the Report noted at that time, "...new trade agreements, such as the Central American Free Trade Agreement (CAFTA), provide an opportunity for the transshipment of Chinese textiles through third country ports, which would undermine the China specific textile safeguards imposed by the U.S. against a range of Chinese goods in December."[27]

The USCC raised this issue again in its 2008 Annual Report, in its analysis of the impact of Chinese imports upon import-sensitive product lines in the Gulf of Mexico regions of the United States after China's admission to the WTO,

> Antidumping penalties imposed by the United States on Chinese shrimp and crawfish exports sold at below market value accomplished little of their intended effect. This appears to be due in part to transshipment by China through ports of other Asian nations in order to avoid the penalty tariffs and in part to the failure to collect the penalty tariffs." [28]
>
> ...a penalty tariff was imposed on shrimp from China and five other countries beginning in 2005... At first, the penalty tariffs seemed to be working to the benefit of U.S. shrimpers. Frozen shrimp imports from China dropped from about 120 million pounds in 2004 to 25 million pounds in 2005... [However,] Louisiana dockside prices of wild-caught shrimp... stayed relatively flat... Imported shrimp's major effect on the U.S. market was to drive the price lower and then to help keep it there, despite the tariff. The U.S. industry... has blamed this, in part, on the Chinese practice of transshipping shrimp through ports in other countries to escape the penalty tariff.

For example, shrimp exports suddenly began arriving in the United States from Papua New Guinea, a country that had not previously exported any shrimp. Shrimp exports from Indonesia and Malaysia also showed large increases. Cambodia, which had exported no shrimp to the United States and had imported none from China, suddenly imported nearly 2 million pounds from China and exported more than 3.5 million pounds to the United States in the weeks after the preliminary Department of Commerce antidumping ruling against China in July 2004." [29]

Another means of evading levies is to relocate production to a third country. While such production no longer is reflected in Chinese export figures to America, they nevertheless reflect the activities of Chinese companies. A key example of this is furniture. In January 2005, the Commerce Department imposed an import tariff on Chinese-made beds, nightstands and related goods. In response, Chinese furniture makers (mostly Taiwanese businessmen who had set up factories in Dongguan, China) opened factories in Vietnam. Vietnam is now the biggest source of wooden bedroom furniture sold in America, and these furniture makers are now considering expanding production to Indonesia. As a result,

> imports now account for about 70 percent of the U.S. market for beds and similar items, up from 58 percent before Washington intervened to try to protect domestic manufacturers from Chinese 'dumping' or the export of goods at unfairly low prices... The number of Americans now employed making bedroom furniture is less than half what it was when the tariff began.[30]

Basic Composition of U.S. Exports to China

All of the top six U.S. export categories to China in 2011 were the same categories as in 2000. Exports in each of these key categories have grown in absolute terms from 2000 to 2011 (see Figures 2, 3 and 4).

The top export categories[31] from the U.S. to China in 2000 were:

1.	Computer and Electronic Products	2.	Chemicals
3.	Transportation Equipment	4.	Machinery, except electrical
5.	Agricultural Products	6.	Waste and Scrap

In comparison, the top export categories[32] from the U.S. to China in 2011 were:

1.	Agricultural Products	2.	Computer and Electronic Products
3.	Chemicals	4.	Transportation Equipment
5.	Waste and Scrap	6.	Machinery, except electrical

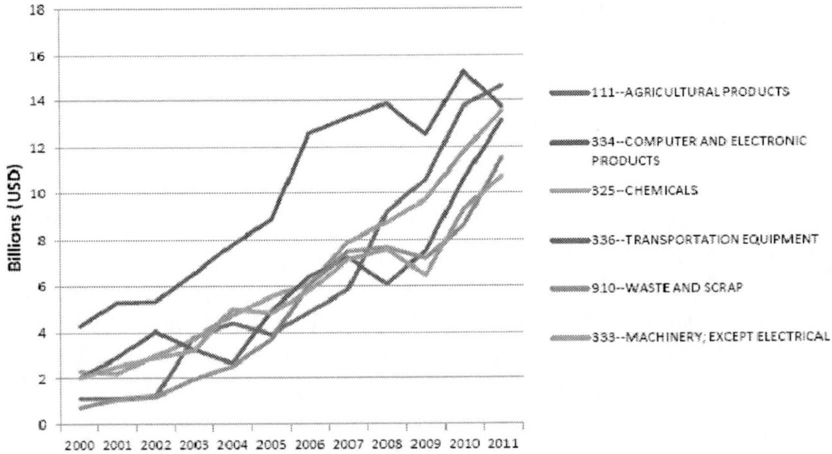

Figure 2. Exports from U.S to China (2000 - 2011, NAICS 3-digit).

The most striking change in the period from 2000 to 2011 is the growing relative importance of the two categories of non-manufactured goods (agricultural products and waste/scrap) among the top six export categories. Agricultural products have gone from being the 5th largest U.S. export to China in 2000 to the largest export category 8in 2011. Since 2006, waste and scrap has been a top-five export every year except 2010, when it was the 6th largest U.S. export to China.

This illustrates a larger trend within this period regarding U.S. exports to China: Approximately 84.5 percent of U.S. exports to China in 2000 were classified as manufactured goods, versus only 68.7 percent in 2011. Concurrently, U.S. exports of non-manufactured goods exploded from $2.5 billion (approximately 15 percent of exports) in 2000 to $32.6 billion (approximately 31 percent of exports) in 2011. This means that the relative share of non-manufactured goods exported from the U.S. to China roughly doubled from 2000 to 2011, and the absolute value increased 13-fold.[33] To better understand these trends, this report next turns to examining these top export categories, divided into non-manufactured versus manufactured goods.

NON-MANUFACTURED GOODS

One obvious change in U.S.-China trade since China entered the WTO is that the United States ran a trade surplus with China of $23.8 billion in non-manufactured goods in 2011 versus a deficit of $283 million in 2000.[34] This surplus in 2011 was almost entirely derived from two sectors: agriculture, and waste and scrap. (See Figure 5)

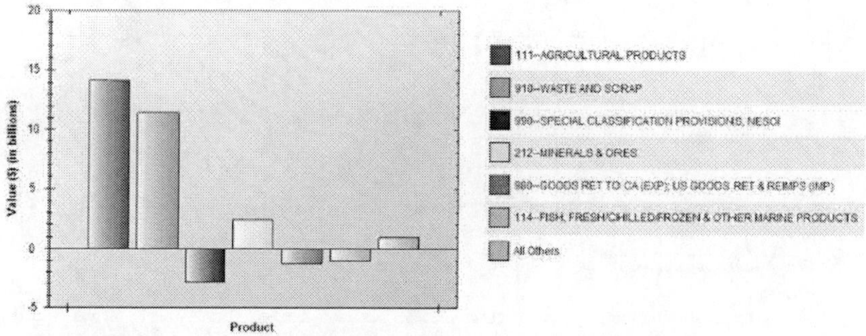

Figure 3. 2011 Balances with China for NAICS All Non-Manufactured Goods.

Agriculture and waste materials are not the only two categories of non-manufactured goods in which exports increased between 2000 and 2011. Exports of oil, gas, minerals and ores from the United States to China also grew substantially over this period: from $105 million in 2000 to $2.6 billion in 2011. In particular, metal ore exports grew from $32.9 million in 2000 to $1.5 billion in 2011, and coal and petroleum gas exports went from a mere $540,985 in 2000 to over $835 million in 2011.[35]

Agricultural Products

Plant-based agricultural products, as distinct from livestock products, made up the lion's share of U.S. agricultural exports to China between 2000 and 2011. (See Figure 4: About 85.3 percent of agriculture and livestock product exports in 2011 were plant-based agricultural products.) Agricultural products roughly doubled as a share of all U.S. exports to China (from 7.1 percent in 2000 to 14.1 percent in 2011– see Figures 2 and 3). China became the top U.S. agricultural products export market in 2010.[36] After failing to achieve sustained growth in the 1990s, exports of American agricultural products to China have increased especially sharply since 2002 (see Figure 4). The value of agricultural exports from the United States to China went from $1.2 billion in 2000 to $14.7 billion in 2011.

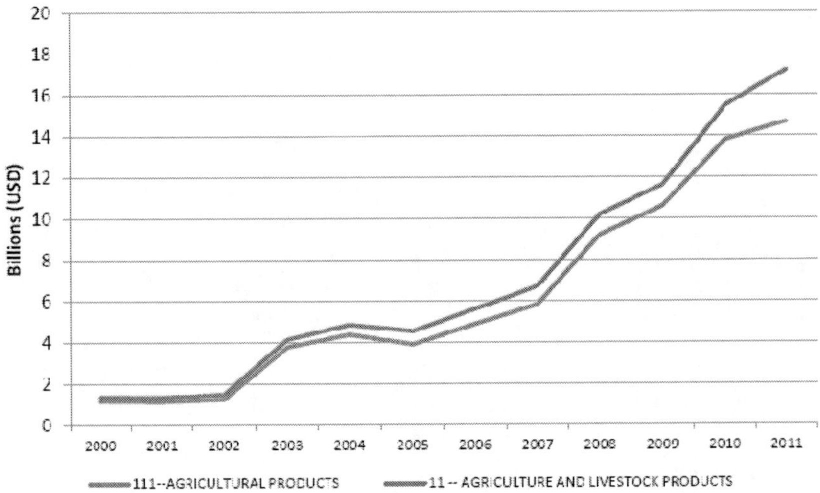

Figure 4. Agriculture and Livestock Products Exports, U.S. to China (2000-2011, NAICS 3-digit).

The single most significant factor observable in U.S. agricultural exports to China is the dramatic growth in soybean sales, which rose from roughly $1 billion in 2000 to $10.5 billion in 2011. Soybeans not only stand out amongst agricultural exports to China, but have achieved an increasingly dominant position among total U.S. exports to China since 2000. Since 2008 soybeans have been the single largest export from the United States to China (see Figure 5), with U.S. companies shipping $10.5 billion worth of soybeans to China in the year 2011.[37]

In part because of increased United States - China soybean trade, China is now the world's largest soybean importer and the United States is the world's top exporter.[39] This trend of heavy Chinese purchases of soybeans from other countries is likely to increase in the future rather than reverse itself, since according to Xiaoping Zhang, acting director in China for the U.S. Soybean

Export Council, "most of the land in China that can be farmed profitably is under cultivation and that available land is shrinking in the face of development."[40]

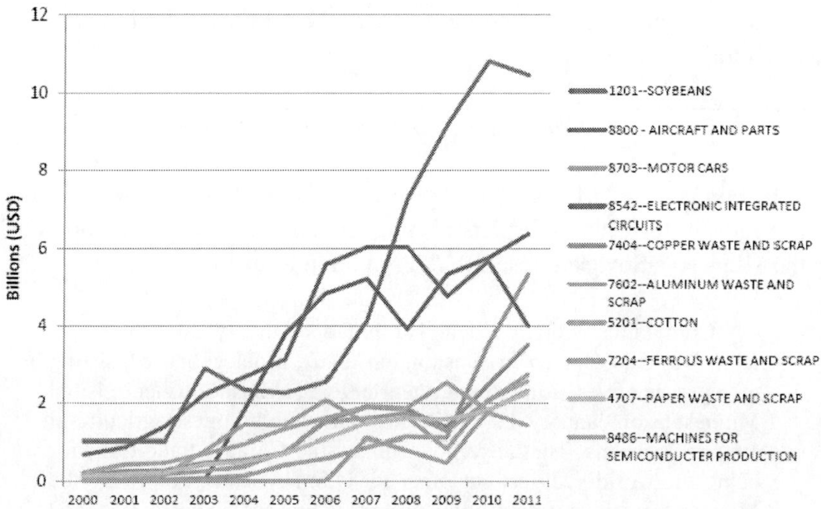

Figure 5. Top U.S. Exports to China (2000 – 2011, HS 4-Digit).[38]

China currently buys approximately a third of America's annual soybean crop[41] for use in animal feed and other important food products like cooking oil.[42] The political sensitivity of inflated food prices in China and the high percentage of soybean demand satisfied through trade with the U.S. has greatly increased China's vulnerability to shocks in U.S. supply. The extent of interdependence between the U.S. and Chinese markets has become especially evident as a result of serious drought conditions in 2012 throughout the American Midwest and Great Plains regions. In August 2012, the U.S. Department of Agriculture (USDA) reported that U.S. soybean growing conditions were the worst since 1988, and reduced its annual crop estimate to 4.2 billion bushels (16 percent below 2011's record-setting crop levels).[43] The drought further depressed already eroded global inventories and prompted market prices to skyrocket to over $17 a bushel in the final weeks of August.[44]

Despite the efforts of U.S. soybean farm leaders to reassure Chinese customers of their stability, Chinese buyers responded by cancelling 163,000 tons of soybean purchases in summer 2012, reducing net sales to their lowest levels in over a year.[45] In an effort to diversify its sources of supply, China has also emerged as a major customer for soybeans grown in South American nations, particularly Brazil and Argentina. As of November 2012, there were signs that Brazil could overtake the position of the United States as China's largest supplier of soybeans — due both to record harvests in Brazil, as well as to the spike in prices for U.S. soybeans caused by drought conditions in many agricultural states.[46]

Minnesota's Soybean Sales to China

Making a pilgrimage to America's heartland is fast becoming a prerequisite for Chinese leaders visiting the United States. As reported by the Minnesota Soybean Research & Promotion Council,

> Coinciding with President Hu Jintao's January 2011 meetings with President Obama in Washington, D.C., a delegation consisting of representatives from China's ten largest soybean crushers visited Minnesota on January 19th to discuss the state's largest agricultural export: soybeans. The Governor thanked the Chinese trade team for being the world's largest customer for U.S. soybeans. Following the Minnesota visit, the delegation went to Chicago where they signed commitments to purchase more than 423 million bushels of U.S. soybeans valued at $6.68 billion. [47]

According to some sources, China's difficulty feeding itself will present an increasing number of opportunities for American farmers.[48] Recent soybean contracts "also underscore the growing importance of US grain exports to the world's largest country, which is expected to surpass Mexico this year as the second-largest buyer of US farm products. China needs to import increasing volumes of protein-rich food to feed its swelling urban ranks." [49] As was said by one farmer, "China is extremely important to Minnesota agriculture, especially soybean farmers. Look at a Minnesota soybean field and realize that every fourth row is purchased by China." [50]

In February 2012, then-PRC Vice President Xi Jinping visited Iowa during his tour of the United States.

The stopover was part homecoming: Xi visited Muscatine, Iowa in 1985 as part of an agricultural research delegation, and he met with the family that hosted him on that first trip. However, Xi also sought to highlight one sector of U.S.-China bilateral trade that unambiguously favors the United States.

Soybean exports from Iowa to China increased 13-fold from 2000 to 2010, according to the Iowa Department of Agriculture.[51] Perhaps most important of all to Iowa's agricultural sector, the Chinese delegation signed agreements to purchase 8.62 million metric tons of soybeans (worth $4.3 billion) from farmers in the state.[52]

Although soybeans have been the mainstay of U.S. agricultural exports to China, the past decade has also seen increases in exports of other agricultural and livestock products, to include cotton, fish & seafood, and meat (see Figure 6).

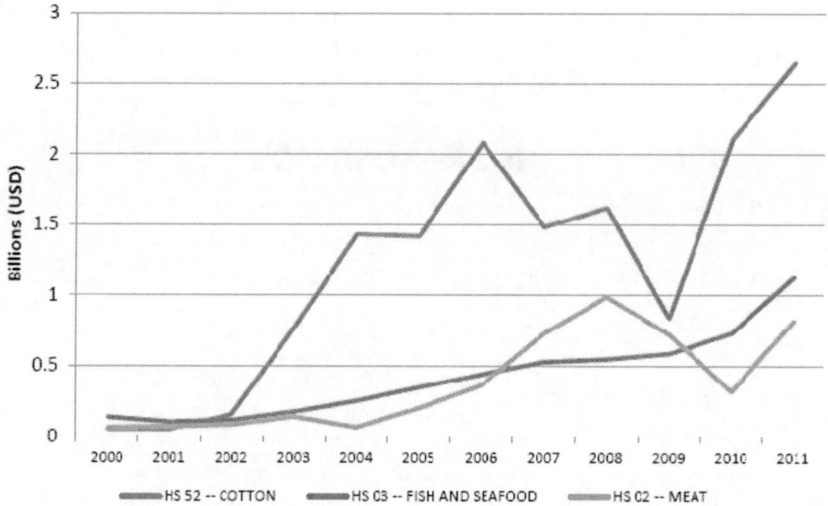

Figure 6. Exports of Selected Agricultural Products (Cotton, Seafood, and Meat) from the United States to China (2000 – 2011) .

Other particular U.S. agricultural sectors have also seen significant growth in exports to China since 2000. A key example of a U.S. agricultural product that may have directly benefited from China's accession to the WTO is tobacco.[56] According to an article in 2007 published by *Tobacco International*,[57] "the boost for imports of leaf tobacco began when the import duty dropped to 10 percent according to WTO guidelines in 2004, compared with the previous duty of 40 percent."[58]

"Back Door" Beef Exports to China

The uneven increase in U.S. sales of meat to China during this period is striking because China has still not lifted its ban on U.S. beef.[53]

However, some analysts claim that lifting this official ban on beef would not provide significant new Chinese market access for American beef exporters, due to existent "back door" exports of U.S. beef to China as transshipped via Hong Kong.

The commodity research and consulting firm Allendale Inc.[54] has published a chart showing that "the volume of U.S. beef shipped to China through the back door of Hong Kong has increased from about 50 million pounds in 2003 to almost 125 million pounds in 2010. As stated by a company official, 'The message to us is (don't) expect beef exports to China to explode if a deal goes through'."[55]

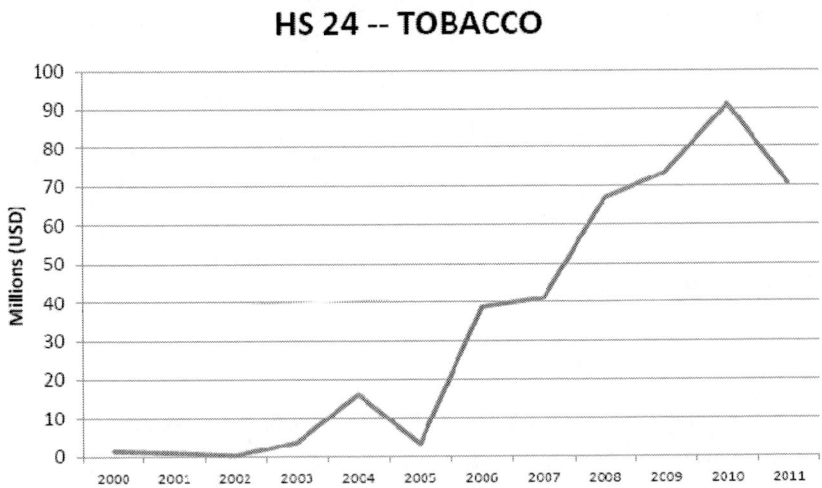

Figure 7. U.S. Tobacco Exports to China (2000-2011, HS 2-digit).

U.S. tobacco exports to China have skyrocketed since 2005 (see Figure 7). Exports have increased by over 60 times, from $2.5 million in 2000 to $117 million in 2011. Notably, this increase has consisted almost entirely of unmanufactured tobacco,[59] as opposed to finished tobacco products like cigarettes. China is the world's biggest cigarette market by volume, but maintains high tariffs for imported manufactured cigarettes and other finished tobacco products.[60]

Not all agricultural exports grew consistently from 2000 to 2011. Cereal exports to China had an uneven decade, with wheat and meslin exports in particular failing to sustain substantial growth (see Figure 8). This may be related to China's national policy of encouraging autarkic self-sufficiency in human staple consumption grains. According to Keith Bradsher, Hong Kong bureau chief of *The New York Times*, "China has been essentially self-sufficient in grain for decades, for national security reasons... China's national obsession with self-sufficiency in food includes corn, another crop that is grown and consumed entirely in China with minimal imports or exports." [61] Despite Mr. Bradsher's claim, there has recently been growth in U.S. exports of corn to China, especially between 2009 – 2011 (see Figure 8), and some analysts argue that China will increasingly import corn and wheat to keep up with internal demand. [62]

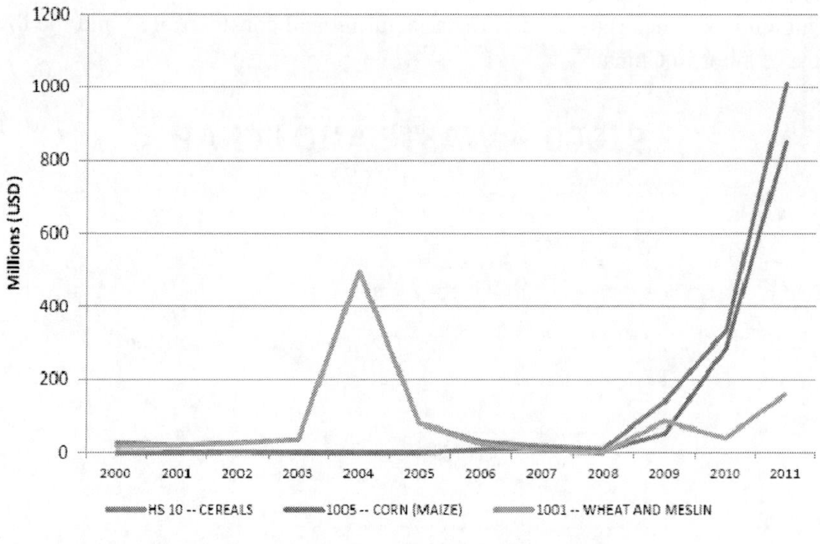

Figure 8. Cereal Exports, U.S. to China (2000-2011, HS 4-Digit).

Waste and Scrap

After China entered the WTO, the value of U.S. waste and scrap exports to China increased more than 15-fold, from $740 million in 2000 to $11.5 billion in 2011, and more than doubled as a share of U.S. exports to China (from 4.6 percent in 2000 to 11.1 percent in 2011– see Figures 2 and 3). This increase was mainly driven by ferrous metal, paper, copper, and aluminum waste / scrap. In 2011, waste and scrap was still the second largest non-manufactured U.S. export category to China, behind only agriculture. Waste and scrap had an especially prominent position in U.S. exports to China from 2006 to 2009. For example, of the top ten exports from the United States to China in 2009, numbers 4 through 7 were all waste products[63]:

4. Ferrous waste and scrap – $2.51 billion in sales
5. Paper waste and scrap – $1.57 billion in sales
6. Copper waste and scrap – $1.36 billion in sales
7. Aluminum waste and scrap – $1.26 billion in sales[64]

The increase in waste and scrap exports during this period was likely driven by a combination of high commodity prices, strong demand within China for raw materials used in manufacturing and construction,[65] and the low cost of labor in China.[66]

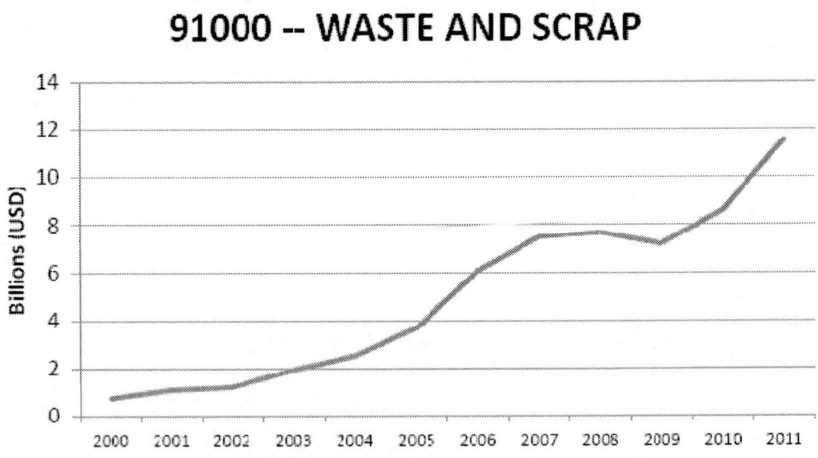

Figure 9. Exports (Waste and Scrap, NAICS 910), U.S. to China (2000-2011, NAICS 3-digit).

Since scrap is a low-value product, exporting scrap has involved large volumes of waste going from the United States to China each year. [68] Based upon the high volumes of waste and scrap exported from the U.S. to China, some commentators have drawn strong conclusions. For example, in 2010 Clyde Prestowitz of the Economic Strategy Institute wrote in the *Huffington*

Post: "If you want to know what's wrong with America and why record numbers of Americans are telling the pollsters that they're fed up, just take a look at how we trade with China. Our major import is nearly $50 billion of computer equipment while our major export is about $8 billion of waste paper and scrap metal. Yes, that's right. We're swapping garbage for computers with China – and lots of other countries as well."[69]

Portrait of a Scrap Dealer
(excerpt from 2004 New York Times article)

"China is very hungry," said David Pan, a Chinese-born scrap metal buyer, as a truck carrying steel reinforcing bars from a dismantled building in San Diego prepared to dump its cargo with a deafening clatter on the floor of his warehouse in Maywood, an industrial town just south of here. "They need a lot of material."

A decade ago, Mr. Pan was working in a Los Angeles restaurant when relatives back in China asked him to start buying scrap. Now, as China booms, so does Mr. Pan's business, called Universal Scrap Metals. He ships about 500 containers a month to China filled with battered pipes, fine metal shavings, doorknobs, jumbles of wire, crumpled cars and all other manner of flotsam. He is even negotiating to buy the remains of a steel factory in Utah; he would ship it, as scrap, to his native country. American scrap dealers, an industry of 1,200 or so mainly mom-and-pop operations, are sharing in the boom times. [67]

Excerpted from Andrew Pollack and Keith Bradsher, "China's Need for Metal Keeps U.S. Scrap Dealers Scrounging," The New York Times, March 13, 2004.

Likely as a result of the global financial crisis, scrap exports from the United States to China slowed down in 2008 and 2009 (see Figure 9). According to Guan Aiguo, Chairman of the China Resource Recycling Association, "Falling material prices on the international market and fewer bulk commodity transactions, plus weakening export and domestic demand, dragged down waste prices [in 2008]." [70]

Most notably, copper and aluminum scrap exports to China in 2009 dropped to pre-2006 levels.[71] However, scrap exports have rebounded in the last two years, jumping from $7.2 billion in 2009 to $11.5 billion in 2011.

The Dangers of Relying upon Waste
(excerpt from 2009 New York Times article)

As of 2009, the multibillion-dollar recycling industry had gone into a nosedive because of the global economic crisis and a concomitant fall in commodity prices. As a result, American and European waste dealers who sell to China are finding that their shipments are being refused by clients when they arrive in Asia. The drop in commodity prices was so rapid that in a matter of weeks container ships carrying used railroad wheels and empty dog food cans arrived in Chinese ports worth far less than they had been when they departed Newark, Rotterdam or Los Angeles.

"Everything was moving along just fine until October and then we fell off a cliff," said Bruce Savage, a spokesman for the Institute of Scrap Recycling Industries, a trade organization that mostly represents American waste processing companies. The United States exported $22 billion worth of recycled materials to 152 countries in 2007. Now the organization estimates the value of American recyclables has decreased by 50 to 70 percent. Western dealers say they are grappling with mounting stockpiles whose value in many cases continues to sink. To make matters worse, Chinese importers have been demanding to renegotiate contracts drastically downward. In some cases, they are refusing to accept shipments they already have a contractual obligation to take.

"There are still many containers full of waste sitting at the port in Hong Kong," Mr. Wang, of China National Resources Recycling Association, said. "It's hard to say when they'll be picked up." According to the association, a ton of copper scrap now sells for $3,000, down from more than $8,000 in 2007. Tin is now selling for $5 a pound, down from $300. Paper has sagged by as much as 80 percent. "People in this industry were once making a killing taking waste from overseas, but the era of huge profits is now over," Mr. Wang said.

Now waste traders in the United States are shutting mills, cutting production and selling their stock at fire-sale prices. George Adams, president of SA Recycling, which processes metal at 40 recycling plants in the western United States, said he wrote down $10 million in losses in October. 'That inventory is gone now, but the pain I won't soon forget,' said Mr. Adams, who ships much of his product to China.[72]

Excerpted from Dan Levin, "China's Big Recycling Market Is Sagging," The New York Times, March 11, 2009.

Manufactured Goods

The share of manufactured goods in U.S. exports to China decreased from around 84.5 percent in 2000 to 68.7 percent in 2011.[73] The U.S. runs a major trade deficit with China in terms of manufactured goods, which has grown substantially from 2000 to 2011. The primary source of this deficit is computer and electronic products. Among major U.S. manufactured exports to China, the only U.S. trade surplus is a modest surplus in the category of transportation equipment (see Figure 10).[74]

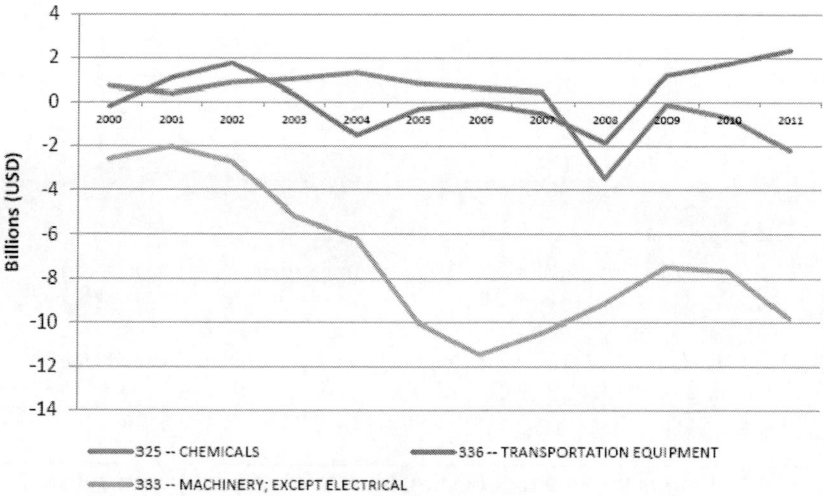

Figure 10. Trade Balance (Major U.S. Exports, except Computers and Electronics), U.S. and China (2000-2011), NAICS 3-digit.

Compared with the massive trade deficit in computer and electronic products and in manufactured goods more generally, the significance of the small surplus in transportation equipment is marginal at best (see Figure 11).

One potential explanation for the growing imbalance between the U.S. and China in manufactured imports and exports is that "U.S. manufacturers have abandoned products with thin profit margins, like consumer electronics, toys and shoes. They've ceded that sector to China, Indonesia and other emerging nations with low labor costs. Instead, American factories have seized upon complex and expensive goods requiring specialized labor: industrial lathes, computer chips, fighter jets, health care products."[75] To test this hypothesis and better understand the composition of major U.S. manufactured goods exported to China, this paper will now examine the top three categories of manufactured products exported from the United States to China in greater detail.

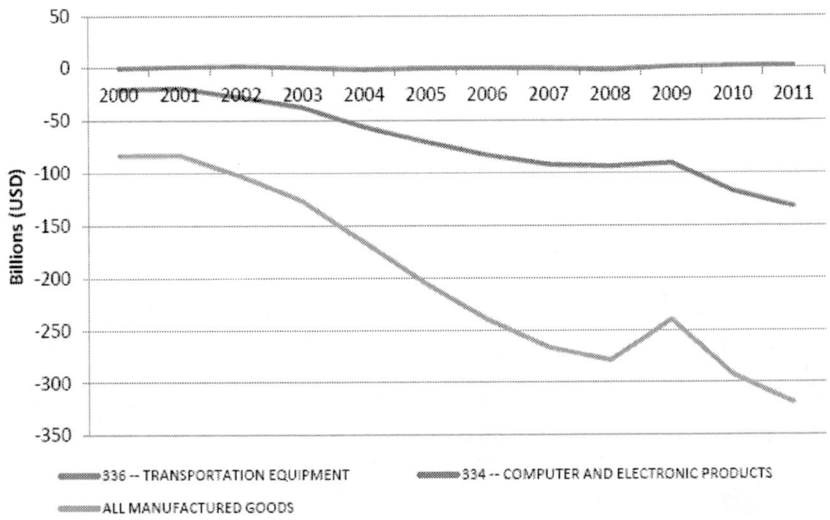

Figure 11. Trade Balance (Transportation Equipment vs. All Manufactured Goods), U.S. and China (2000-2011, NAICS, 3-digit).

What is the Impact of U.S.-China Trade on American Jobs?

According to the U.S. Bureau of Labor Statistics, the number of U.S. manufacturing jobs fell from 12.2 million to 8.1 million during the past decade; this represents more jobs lost in the manufacturing sector than in the previous two decades combined. From the first quarter of 2001 to the first quarter of 2010, 39 percent of U.S. manufacturing plants with over 250 employees closed.[76] A transition in the United States from exporting manufactured to non-manufactured goods, coupled with increased imports of manufactured goods from China, has almost certainly negatively impacted production capacity and employment levels in a number of U.S. manufacturing industries. However, it has also directly and indirectly created jobs in sectors that have benefitted from more open trade with China. It is difficult to accurately estimate the net number of jobs lost and created as a result of increased trade between the United States and China.

Furthermore, existing research on this issue may be heavily influenced by ideological outlook or institutional interests. According to Clyde Prestowitz of the Economic Strategy Institute, there is no doubt that American manufacturing decline is closely associated with China's manufacturing rise:

> From 24 percent of GDP in 1980, manufacturing has fallen by more than half to less than 12 percent of GDP today. To some extent this is a natural development as all developed countries tend to create larger service sectors as their economies mature. But the relative shrinkage of the U.S. manufacturing sector has been extreme in comparison to countries such as Japan (18.3 percent of GDP), Germany (22 percent), France (15 percent), and even the UK (13 percent).
>
> The U.S. decline has been particularly brutal in the past eight years, during which it has lost about a third (from 17 percent to 11.8 percent) of its share of GDP as 40,000 manufacturing plants closed their doors.
>
> For instance, the American steel industry that produced 97.4 million tons in 1999 managed to do only 91.5 million tons in 2008 even as Chinese production rose from 124 million to 500 million tons over the same period.
>
> Between 2000 and 2008, 270 major U.S. furniture factories closed as the industry lost 60 percent of its production capacity and the market share of imports rose from 38 percent to nearly 70 percent. The U.S. machine tool industry—the backbone of any industrial economy and essential to defense production—produced only $3.6 billion in equipment, less than 5 percent of world production, down 30 percent from 1998, and only about half of U.S. consumption. In contrast, Germany, Japan, and even Italy currently produce more machine tools than the United States. Chemical plants are another essential element of an industrial economy. In 2008, 80 major plants costing in excess of $1 billion were being constructed somewhere in the world. None of them was being constructed in the United States.[77]

According to Dr. Robert Scott of the Economic Policy Institute, a think tank associated with the U.S. labor union movement, between 2001 and 2011, the U.S.-China trade deficit "eliminated or displaced more than 2.7 million U.S. jobs, over 2.1 million of which (76.9 percent) were in manufacturing."[78]

According to Scott's analysis, 1,064,800 U.S. jobs in computer and electronic products were lost during this period.

Other hard-hit sectors include apparel and accessories (211,200 jobs), miscellaneous manufactured goods (111,800), and fabricated metal products (120,600). Several service sectors were also hard hit by indirect job losses, including administrative, support and waste management services (160,600) and professional, scientific, and technical services (145,000).[79] The overall job loss calculation in this 2012 study (approximately 2.7 million jobs) is lower than figures released by the Economic Policy Institute in its 2011 report, which estimated a overall loss of 2.8 million U.S. jobs between 2000 and 2010.[80]

There have been a wide range of responses to this critical analysis. Daniel J. Ikenson of the libertarian, pro-free trade Cato Institute counters that "EPI's methodology is not taken seriously by most economists because it approximates job gains from export value and job losses from import value, as though there were a straight line correlation between the figures. And it pretends that imports do not create or support U.S. jobs."[81]

In a similar vein, Dr. Penelope Prime of Mercer University explains that to measure the impact of trade on employment, one cannot simply identify imports as a job-destroying aspect of trade, and exports as a job-creating facet of trade. For example, there are jobs connected to imports, as well as jobs connected with capital flows and government services. Moreover, it is difficult to separate out jobs lost as a result of trade with China from jobs lost as a result of technological change over the past decade. Prime ultimately contends that trade with China has caused employment in the United States both to grow and to shrink, depending upon the type of job in question: i.e. fewer manufacturing jobs and more service related jobs.[82]

An even more positive view of the U.S.-China trade relationship is taken by *Future of U.S. China Trade.com*.[83] According to this organization, "Between 1978 and 2008, the real value of goods and services imported to the United States increased 482 percent, from $328 billion to $1.9 trillion (in 2000 dollars) – reflecting the dramatic increase in global economic integration. At the same time, people in America got much richer; real GDP expanded by 132 percent and total civilian employment rose by 49.3 million jobs."[84]

That said, Scott and Prestowitz are not alone in believing that current trends in U.S. trade with China have had a negative net impact upon jobs. For example, looking not at import and export figures but at currency valuation, other economists have assessed that the undervaluation of China's renminbi has had a serious negative impact on U.S. employment.

For example, Fred Bergsten, the director of the Peterson Institute for International Economics, has estimated that every "$1 billion of exports supports about 6,000 to 8,000 (mainly high-paying manufacturing) jobs in the United States," and that therefore "a trade correction [RMB revaluation] would generate an additional 600,000 to 1.2 million jobs." [85]

Computers and Electronic Products

Exports of computers and electronic products from the United States to China have grown more than three-fold, from a value of $4.2 billion in 2000 to $13.7 billion in 2011. However, the composition of these exports has shifted dramatically over this period – away from assembled products, and towards sales of individual components such as semi-conductors.[86] There has also been growth in exports of measuring and control instruments, which can also be used as components in electronic products (see Figure 12).

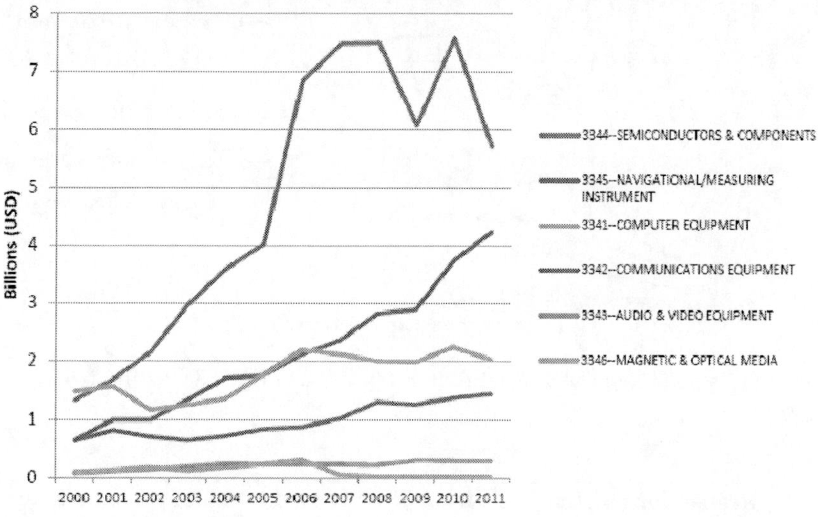

Figure 12. Exports (Computers and Electronics), U.S. to China (2000-2011, NAICS 4-digit).

According to an October 2009 report by research staff at the United States International Trade Commission, "Semiconductors dominate [high-tech exports], representing about 90 percent of U.S. electronic advanced technology product (ATP) exports to China in 2008. Information & communication goods have also been a prominent type of U.S. ATP exports to China. Machine parts, voice and data imaging machines and parts, processing and phone parts make up the products in that category grouping. Taken together, such products can be broadly considered intermediary goods that the United States ships to China as components for final assembly of other products."[87]

At the same time that U.S. exports of computer and electronics intermediary goods have increased to China, computers and electronics imports from China have grown from $24.7 billion to $145.8 billion from 2000 to 2011. This growth has been fueled primarily not by intermediary goods or components from China, but by computer equipment[88] (e.g. laptops), communications equipment (e.g. mobile phones) and audio & video equipment (e.g. televisions) (see Figure 13).

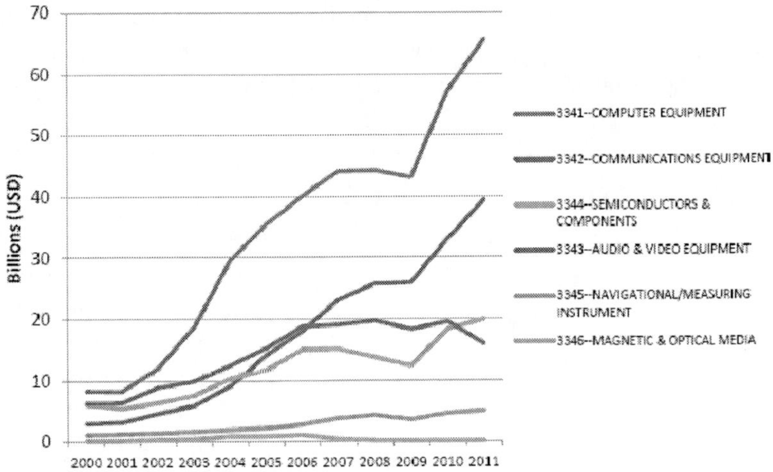

Figure 13. Imports (Computers and Electronics), China to U.S. (2000-2011, NAICS 4-digit).

Restrictions on Sales of "Dual-Use" High Technology Products to China

Chinese officials have asserted that the U.S.-China trade imbalance in high-tech equipment is not solely derived from market forces, but also reflects U.S. export restrictions on certain high-tech products – and that a relaxation of U.S. export controls would help to correct the immense bilateral trade deficit.[90]

This is a complex and controversial point, which has drawn both critics and supporters.

Unlike export controls in many other countries, "in the United States, for the most part, export control policy centers around limitations on exports of advanced technologies (also called 'dual-use' technologies) that could be used to compromise U.S. national security."[91] Dual use technologies are technologies that potentially have both civilian and military applications.

To "ease regulatory burdens for US exporters that seek to tap the enormous China market," the U.S. Department of Commerce introduced the "Validated End User" (VEU) authorization program in 2008.[92] The full implementation of the program for China was announced on January 13, 2009, and "permits civilian companies in China, who pass a rigorous national security review and agree to strict follow-on compliance obligations, to receive under a VEU-specific authorization the same U.S.-controlled items they could previously receive under individual Commerce Department licenses."[93] Critics of the program have challenged such moves on national security grounds, as in June 2009 when Rep. Edward Markey (MA-7) asserted that the program did an inadequate job of investigating the backgrounds of Chinese companies, and that it could undermine international counter-proliferation initiatives.[94]

The Obama administration has expressed a commitment to reforming the export control system. In May 2010, then-U.S. Commerce Secretary Gary Locke told students at China's Tsinghua University that "the Obama administration was moving to ease restrictions on exports of high-technology goods to China."[95] According to a speech by Mr. Locke given on August 31, 2010 in Washington D.C., "We are taking important steps towards streamlining and simplifying our export control system... what we've found so far is that about 74 percent of the licensing activity is for parts and components – items like brake pads and the pivot blocks... which, going forward, will likely be moved to the Commerce Control List or decontrolled...

A reformed export control system will allow us to focus on the high-risk dual-use technologies that pose the greatest risk to our national security, while permitting greater exports of items that pose little or no risk."[96]

President Obama spoke on December 9 of the need to reduce the number of sensitive U.S. military and dual-use items restricted for export. Wes Bush, President of the Northrop Grumman Corporation, said:

"This action will improve the functioning of the government and protect sensitive and critical U.S. technologies while enhancing industry's ability to compete in global markets."[97] Similarly, the National Association of Manufacturers "praised Obama's announcement and said the Milken Institute predicted that modernizing the controls could increase exports in high-value areas and enhance real GDP by $64.2 billion, create 160,000 manufacturing jobs and raise total employment by 340,000 jobs by 2019."[98]

However, there are also skeptics of the potential impact of "dual use" export control reforms upon the trade deficit. As stated in a March 2010 op-ed by Kevin L. Kearns, President of the U.S. Business and Industry Council, these "controls affect only a tiny fraction of U.S. exports. At the heart of the companies' complaints are exports to China and 21 other countries of civilian products with possible military uses – the so-called dual-use exports. According to the latest (2007) U.S. government data, however, total U.S. exports to these countries came to only 6.9 percent of total U.S. exports. And of all the exports to these 'controlled destinations,' a bare 0.8 percent required a Commerce Department license. So the job and growth effects of U.S. export controls clearly are minimal."[99]

Overall, the U.S.-China trade imbalance in computers and electronics grew markedly between 2000 and 2011, rising from $20.5 billion in 2000 to $132.1 billion in 2011. Since computer and electronics products are the 2nd largest U.S. export to China and the top U.S. import from China, it seems possible that this imbalance was partially fueled by components first exported (directly or indirectly) from the United States to China, and then re-imported to the U.S. as parts of assembled computers and other electronics products (notebooks, cell phones, televisions, etc.). According to Derek Scissors of the Heritage Foundation, "The U.S. and PRC are both part of the global production chain in advanced goods, where the U.S. provides inputs such as semiconductors and measuring devices, which China assembles into computers and audio–visual equipment."[89]

Chemicals

China's accession to the WTO was predicted to positively affect U.S. exports of chemicals to China, due to reductions of tariffs on chemicals. Although the share of chemical exports among all exports from the United

States to China has declined slightly (from 14.3 percent in 2000 to 13 percent in 2011 – see Figures 2 and 3), chemical exports have increased significantly in absolute terms: from $2.3 billion in 2000 to $13.6 billion in 2011 (see Figure 14).

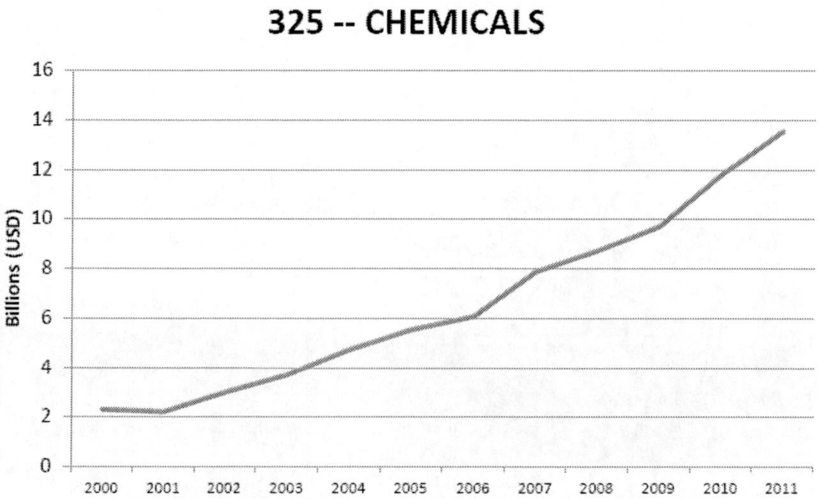

Figure 14. Exports (Chemicals), U.S. to China (2000-2011, NAICS 3-digit).

The composition of U.S. chemical exports to China in 2010 was not reflective of U.S. chemical exports to the world as a whole in 2011 (see Figures 17 and 18). In particular, while 24.5 percent of all U.S. chemical exports to the world in 2011 were composed of pharmaceuticals and medicines, pharmaceuticals make up a mere 9.3 percent of U.S. chemical exports to China (see figures 15 and 16).

(This is not to say that China does not conduct extensive pharmaceutical trade with the U.S. – only that there are limited pharmaceutical exports from the U.S. to China. For a detailed discussion of U.S. imports of pharmaceutical materials from China, see the Commission-sponsored April 2010 report, *Potential Health & Safety Impacts from Pharmaceuticals and Supplements Containing Chinese-Sourced Raw Ingredients.*[100])

The growth in chemical exports from the United States to China from 2000 to 2011 has not been evenly distributed across all categories of chemicals; rather, most of the growth can be attributed to a growth in resin/synthetic rubber and basic chemicals,[101] with moderate growth in other categories such as pesticides and fertilizers (see Figure 17). Combined, these two categories made up 67.4 percent of chemical exports from the U.S. to China in 2011, versus only 57.7 percent in 2000. Since resin and basic chemicals may be used as raw materials, increased U.S. chemical exports from 2000 to 2011 may once again be indicative of China's growing industrial needs.

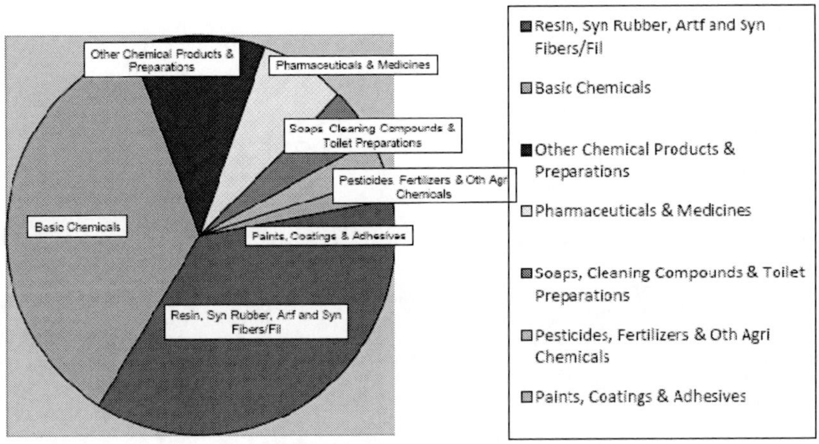

Figure 15. 2011 U.S. Exports to China of NAICS 324 – Chemicals.

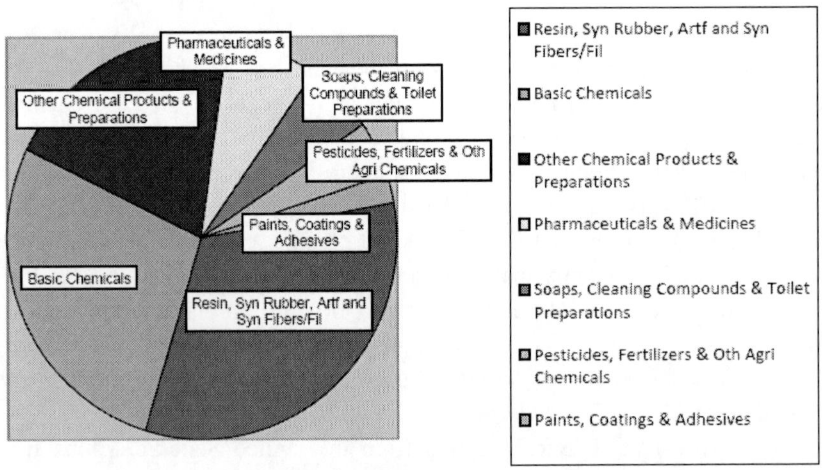

Figure 16. 2011 U.S. Exports to World of NAICS 325 – Chemicals.

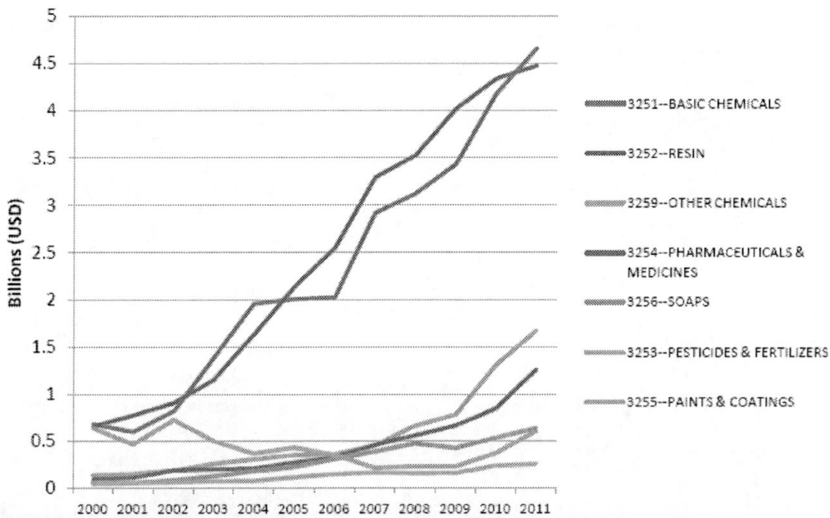

Figure 17. Categories of Chemical Exports, U.S. to China (2000-2011, NAICS 4-digit).

There was a concurrent decline in the percentage share of exports of pesticides, fertilizers and other agricultural chemicals from 2000 to 2010.[102] This is a significant compositional shift because pesticides, fertilizers and other agricultural chemicals were the most important chemical export from the United States to China through most of the 1990s, and were the second largest chemical export from the U.S. to China as of 2000. Fertilizers were not only important amongst chemicals, but were among the Top 10 of all exported products from the U.S. to China from 2000 to 2003 (*see Appendix 1*). This decline was reversed in 2011, when pesticide and fertilizer exports from the United States to China jumped to $602.1 million, up from $368.8 million the previous year *(see chart on the preceding page)*. Whether this increase will be sustained remains to be seen.

TRANSPORTATION EQUIPMENT

The export value of transportation equipment from the United States to China rose from $2 billion in 2000 to $13.2 billion in 2011.[103] While aerospace products and parts have remained the top transportation equipment export category over this period, the most significant change has been the growth of motor vehicle exports. Motor vehicle exports rose from around $41 million in 2000 to $5.4 billion in 2011 (see Figure 18).

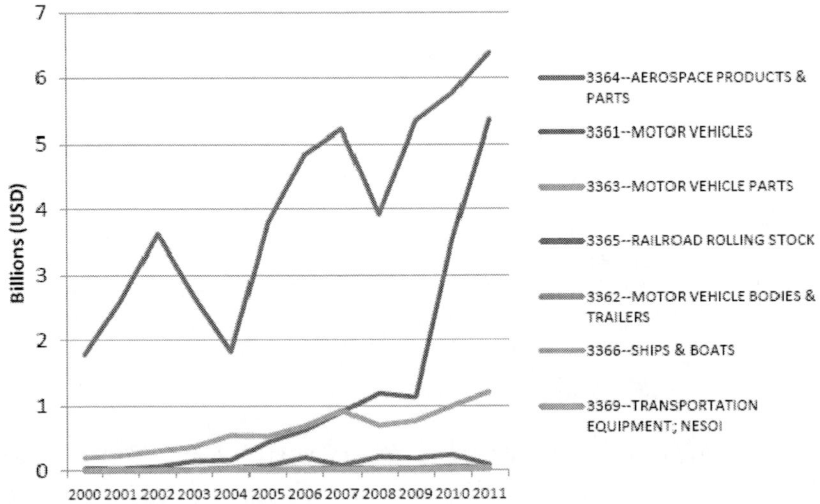

Figure 18. Exports (Transportation Equipment), U.S. to China (2000-2011, NAICS 4-digit).

Aviation

Aerospace production is a pillar industry within American manufacturing. In 2008, the last year for which data was available, more jobs in the United States were supported by exports of U.S. aerospace products than of any other manufacturing or service industry.[104] Aviation comprised 2.8 percent of the nation's manufacturing workforce in 2008, and employed over 500,000 Americans in high-skilled and high-wage jobs.[105] While the relative dominance of aerospace products and parts among transportation products exports has declined in the decade since China's accession to the WTO,[106] aerospace exports remain strong and there is projected continued strong market demand for decades to come.

According to the U.S. Commercial Service, China is now the world's second largest aviation market.[107] The Boeing Corporation has described the growth of the Chinese civil aviation market as follows:

> The number of passengers carried by China's airlines in 2010 was 3.5 times the total in 2000. The in-service jet fleet more than tripled to 1,750 airplanes by 2010, up from 560 airplanes in 2000. In mainland China, the number of commercial aviation airports increased from 139 in 2000 to 175 in 2010. Volumes of passengers, freight, and airplane arrivals and departures at airports in 2010 increased dramatically (4.2, 3.6, and 3.1 times, respectively) over 2000 levels.[108]

In 2010, the Civil Aviation Administration of China (CAAC) projected major continued growth in the Chinese aviation sector through the year 2015, to include the addition of 700 more planes to the civil aviation fleet and the opening of 45 new airports.[109] The Boeing Company has estimated that China will need 3,770 new domestic light civil aircraft (LCA) by 2028, accounting for 42 percent of deliveries to the Asia-Pacific region.[110]

Aircraft and parts[111] (see Appendix 1) have been among the top three exports from the United States to China throughout the period from 2000 to 2011. In 2011, aircraft and parts were the second largest export from the United States to China, behind only soybeans. According to a 2011 *CNN Money* report, these sales are not evenly distributed across the U.S. market — rather, the "Boeing [Corporation] accounts for the lion's share of those sales."[112] According to a report in the *International Business Times*, "Boeing jets are a mainstay in China's air travel and cargo system, representing over 50 percent of all commercial jetliners operating in the country."[113]

Boeing is expected to maintain its market dominance in the immediate future, as "Boeing received final approval on [January 19, 2011] from the Chinese Government confirming a $19 billion aircraft agreement. The contract involves a delivery of 200 aircraft comprising of 737s and 777s over a period of three years (2011-2013)."[114] Addressing their longer term future in China, the Boeing Corporation's *Market Outlook 2010–2029* anticipates that Chinese airlines will purchase about 3,900 new aircraft over the next 20 years for their domestic market. This would roughly triple the size of China's current fleet, valued at $400 billion.[115]

A "Bullet" Aimed at China's Aviation Market?

Some analysts believe that once bullet trains are crisscrossing China, the market for larger airliners will not be as robust as currently projected.[116] However, a 2011 report produced for the Commission by analysts at the RAND Corporation provides conditional support for the Chinese aviation market projections produced by the Boeing Corporation.

High-speed rail is widely expected to pose a serious challenge to the airline industry, at least for travel between China's major coastal urban centers in the east and south of the country. As one analyst observes, the typical air travel time between Shanghai and Beijing, under normal weather conditions, is around 5 hours. The same trip by express high-speed trains would take 5 to 6 hours, without the additional inconveniences necessitated by air travel.

However, the ultimate impact of rail and expanding automotive transit systems on air traffic patterns is more complicated than simple competition between rail and air – there is a real possibility that they might complement one another as well, with business commuters (especially to and from more remote regions) using a combination of rail and air travel to reach their destinations. [117] Based on the analysis of the RAND report, Boeing's projection of a tripling in size of the PRC civilian aviation fleet over the coming two decades appears reasonable, if an average Chinese real growth rate of 7 to 8 percent is assumed to continue over the next two decades.[118]

Does "Indigenous Innovation" Threaten U.S. Aviation Exports?

The current interdependence between a key U.S. export and a single U.S. company (Boeing[119]) carries certain inherent risks. Concerns over these risks are bolstered by China's policy of "indigenous innovation" and an allegedly systematic encouragement of technology transfers through U.S.-Chinese joint ventures. As Thomas Hour and Pankaj Ghemaway have written,

> Just as securing natural resources often drives China's foreign policy, shifting the origination of leading technologies to China is driving the country's industrial policy. In late 2009 China's Ministry of Science and Technology demanded that all the technologies used in products sold to the government be developed in China, which would have forced multinational companies to locate many more of their R&D activities in a country where intellectual property is notoriously unsafe. After howls of protest from foreign governments and companies, the ministry backed down. However, the government still appears intent on creating a tipping point at which multinational companies will have to locate their most-sophisticated R&D projects and facilities in China, enabling it to

eventually catch up with or supplant the United States as the world's most-advanced economy.[120]

According to this understanding of Chinese industrial policy, the situation of German high-speed rail projects in China displays the potential pitfalls of joint ventures with Chinese partner companies, and could presage a similar fate for America's aviation industry. According to Robert Samuelson of *The Washington Post*,

> Initially, foreign firms such as Germany's Siemens got most contracts [for Chinese high-speed rail projects; however] in 2009, the government began requiring foreign firms to enter into minority joint ventures with Chinese companies. Having mastered the 'core technologies,' Chinese companies have captured 80 percent or more of the local market and compete with foreign firms for exports. The same thing is occurring in commercial aircraft.[121]

There is no doubt that there is a clear trend towards foreign aviation companies engaging more deeply in joint ventures with Chinese partners.[122] For example, GE has announced plans to form a joint venture called GE-AVIC Civil Avionics Systems Co., Ltd. In this partnership, GE will supply avionics technology – the electronics that guide the aircraft – for the C919, China's competitor passenger airliner to the Boeing 737 and the Airbus 320.[123] From GE's perspective it is likely simply a question of attempting to expand competencies[124] and improve market share.[125] Despite the long-term risks this might pose for GE, such risks are seen as being par for the course in China, since "doing business in China, often requires Western multinationals like GE to share technology and trade secrets that might eventually enable Chinese companies to beat them at their own game – by making the same products cheaper, if not better."[126]

What makes the GE-AVIC joint venture of particular concern — not just for GE as a company but more broadly for aviation exports from the United States as a whole – is the size and level of government involvement in GE's state-owned partner, China Aviation Industry Corporation (AVIC).[127] According to Clyde Prestowitz, "The deal will result in transfer of most, if not all, of GE's advanced avionics technology to the joint venture with the strong possibility that it will also find its way to AVIC and/or others in China outside the joint venture as other technologies have been doing in similar cases in other industries."[128]

General Electric is by no means alone in supplying aviation technology to China. As James McGregor of APCO puts it, in its desire to

> ...design and manufacture a large commercial aircraft that can compete with Boeing and Airbus... China has set the year 2014 as the target for the first test flight of its home-grown 150-seat airliner, known as the C919... The Chinese government's core strategy for assembling the C919 is to trade market access for technology. Foreign players have been lining up to integrate their technology into the C919 design via technology transfers and joint development. Parker Aerospace, General Electric, Honeywell and Goodrich have all partnered with various Chinese entities or [AVIC]... the Chinese government also envisions the C919 as a global product with a price that will substantially undercut the Boeing 737 and Airbus A320.[129]

The nature of China's political economy allows the Chinese government to apply political and developmental priorities to what, in the United States, might be viewed more narrowly as strictly business decisions. According to an economics writer Steven Pearlstein:

> With its state-controlled economy, China can force its companies to act collaboratively to achieve the country's strategic economic objectives. And that gives it a tremendous advantage in negotiating the terms of trade with a country like ours, where China can strike deals that may provide short-term profits to one company and its shareholders but in the long run undermine the competitiveness of the other country's economy. What's good for GE or Honeywell or Rockwell is [not necessarily] good for America and American workers.[130]

It is possible that some of these concerns (especially related to Chinese firms acquiring most if not all of their U.S. partner's advanced avionics technology) may not impact U.S. aviation exports in the short-term future. According to a recent RAND study commissioned by the U.S.-China Economic and Security Review Commission, "Western companies [who are partnering with Chinese firms] have a vested interest in maintaining control of their core intellectual property, which likely explains why most of the technologies planned for the C919 are, with a few exceptions, already currently deployed in modern airliners."[131] That said, while

> Western aerospace companies have been generally cautious about transferring advanced technology to China or setting up joint ventures in critical areas... a turning point may have been have reached with the

> Commercial Aircraft Corporation of China (COMAC) C919 project... COMAC management has made it explicitly clear that foreign bidders on the C919 program are expected to form joint ventures with Chinese partners, especially in high-technology areas such as advanced materials and flight control systems, where Chinese technology is lagging. In areas of less concern, the Chinese are content with traditional subcontracting or other work-share arrangements, although... local production is considered a minimum requirement for foreign suppliers to the C919 program.[132]

On this topic, the report concludes that "all wide-body aircraft will be imported at least through 2020. Although Chinese airlines will apparently be required to buy at least some C919s, their preference, and that of their customers, will continue to be for Boeing and Airbus aircraft with proven safety and reliability records. If the C919 can establish a comparable safety and reliability record, however, and can offer improved comfort and fuel efficiency, it is possible that, over time, it will begin to take market share away from Boeing and Airbus (provided, of course, that Boeing and Airbus do not bring to market even better aircraft in the meantime)." 133

With decidedly more optimism the report projects that "the markets for cargo aircraft, general aviation, and helicopters in China, although significantly smaller than that for passenger aircraft, are also expected to grow rapidly in the coming years." [134] In particular, with regards to fixed-wing general aviation aircraft, the report states that:

> As of late 2009, the nation's severely restrictive airspace management regime had limited the number of fixed-wing general aviation aircraft in China to about 800 (compared with 230,000 in the United States). Reforms are under way, however, and the number of fixed-wing general aviation aircraft in China is expected to increase by 30 percent per year over the next five to 10 years, resulting in more than 10,000 new aircraft by 2020.[135]
>
> A particularly attractive segment of the general aviation market may be business aviation. According to industry data, as of the end of 2009, there were 50,000 business aircraft in the world, 18,000 of them in the United States alone.
>
> Even a developing country such as Brazil boasted 2,000 business aircraft, whereas China had only 30 in commercial operation at that time... Since China does not appear to have an indigenous business-aircraft development program, all of these aircraft will presumably have to be imported.[136]

Motor Vehicles

The marked growth in U.S. automotive exports to China since 2008 has primarily been in assembled vehicles (as distinct from automotive parts). In 2008 and 2009, motor vehicles were the 10th largest export from the United States to China, and in 2011 became the 3rd largest category (see Appendix 1). According to September 2010 commentary from the Democratic Leadership Council:

> [I]n 2005 American auto plants - including production by Big Three and international car companies – made 11.5 million cars, SUVs and pickup trucks. Of these, 1.9 million went abroad, with 1.15 million going to Canada and Mexico and another 120,000 to Germany. In the crisis year 2009, production fell to 5.6 million, mainly because of the drop in buying at home, while 1.7 million went abroad. If their early figures for 2010 hold up through the fall, production will rebound to about 9.3 million cars and trucks, and exports will jump to 2.5 million.
>
> Some of this reflects reviving sales to Mexico and Canada – but car exports to China are rising at a dramatic rate, with sales tripling in a single year.[137] The jump lifts China above Germany as the 3rd-largest American automobile buyer this year (up from 10th in 2005 and 48th in 2000), the U.S.' largest trade-surplus country for vehicles (though still much more a supplier than buyer of auto parts) – and also lifts China above Japan and Germany as Michigan's third-ranking export market.
>
> The jump has lifted Michigan state exports by 38 percent this year – the fastest growth among the top ten exporting states. The state has picked up about 150,000 jobs this year; its unemployment rate has dropped from 14.5 percent in January to 13.1 percent in August, and from 16 percent to 14 percent around Detroit.[138]

From 2000 to 2011, the export value of motor vehicles from the United States to China has risen around 86 times, from $40.9 million in 2000 to $5.4 billion in 2011. This growth in exports appears to be driven by market forces: "China surpassed the United States as the world's largest automobile market [in 2008]."[139] The Chinese government projects that by 2020, there will be 140 million cars in China (seven times the current level), and that the number of cars sold annually will rise from 8.63 million units (as of 2008) to 20.7 million units (by 2020).[140]

While there are latent dangers that could slow this projected long-term growth (for example, major congestion across large cities in China,[141] a consideration that has already prompted action in cities like Shanghai and

Beijing to attempt to limit the number of new cars on the road[142]), American automakers are active in increasing both sales in, and exports to, the Chinese market. GM in particular has already established such a dominant position in the Chinese market[143] that its sales in China now outpace its sales in the United States.[144] These sales by GM include exports from the United States as well as locally produced vehicles.[145] Ford has also expressed a commitment to further increase exports to China to supplement its Chinese manufacturing operations.[146]

As a "pillar industry," China's domestic automotive industry continues to enjoy preferential government support, as well as state-imposed market access barriers to foreign competition. The industry is also engaged in joint venture and technology transfer arrangements with both U.S. companies (Ford and General Motors) and foreign companies (to include Volkswagen, FIAT, and Toyota).[147] Chinese motor vehicle exports to the U.S. remain modest — these low-tech vehicles are mainly exported to developing countries in Africa, Asia, and the Middle East.[148] Chinese auto parts exports to the United States, however, have increased over the last decade.[149] While there is potential for auto export growth to the United States, the Chinese auto market is fragmented and Chinese vehicle exports face concerns about IPR, safety, and quality.[150]

Controversies Regarding Currency Valuation as a Factor in the U.S.-China Trade Imbalance

The impact of the valuation of the Chinese currency (the *Renminbi,* or RMB) is another widely discussed factor affecting the U.S.-China trade balance. According to the *2010 Annual Report to Congress* of the United States Economic and Security Review Commission,

> China's deliberately undervalued RMB has unfairly conferred substantial economic advantages on China to the detriment of major trading partners, principally the United States and Europe.
>
> China's undervalued RMB makes China's exports cheaper and imports more expensive, and it encourages foreign direct investment into China, resulting in the loss of investment and jobs in Europe and the United States...China's management of its exchange rate regime is a major contributing factor to the U.S. trade deficit with China. The undervaluation of the RMB effectively subsidizes all Chinese exports and places a de facto tariff on all Chinese imports and also incentivizes U.S. companies to outsource production to China.[151]

The USCC is not alone in these conclusions. U.S. Federal Reserve Chairman Ben Bernanke has claimed that the Chinese government's manipulation of its currency effectively subsidizes China's exports.[152] The president of the Peterson Institute of International Economics, Fred Bergsten, has called RMB undervaluation "a blatant form of protectionism . . . which subsidizes all Chinese exports 25 to 40 percent [and] places the equivalent of a 25 to 40 percent tariff on all Chinese imports." [153] According to a research paper released by the Peterson Institute in August 2010, "a 10 percent real effective appreciation of the RMB would lead to a reduction in the U.S. current account deficit of between $22 billion and $63 billion per year..." [154] Central bank governors from other countries, like India and Brazil, have also criticized the RMB's undervaluation.[155]

However, not all analysts agree that *renminbi* undervaluation plays a pivotal role in the U.S.-China trade deficit. For example, while conceding that many economists agree the *renminbi* is undervalued, Daniel Ikenson of the Cato Institute asks the question, "Will *renminbi* appreciation have the intended effect of reducing the bilateral trade deficit?" His conclusion is that "[t]he empirical evidence says it won't." 156 The central thesis of his argument is that:

> On the import side, the evidence is not compelling that an appreciating renminbi deters U.S. consumption of Chinese goods. As the renminbi was growing stronger between 2005 and 2008, U.S. imports from China increased by $94.3 billion, or 38.7 percent. Not only did Americans demonstrate strong price inelasticity, but they actually increased their purchases of Chinese imports, in seeming defiance of the law of demand.
>
> One reason for continued U.S. consumption of Chinese goods despite the relative price increase may be that there is a shortage of substitutes for Chinese-made goods in the U.S. market. In some cases, there are no domestically produced alternatives at all. Accordingly, U.S. consumers were faced with the choice of purchasing higher-priced items from China or forgoing consumption of an item altogether."[157]

In May 2010, a delegation of senior U.S. executives representing the American Chamber of Commerce in Beijing claimed that *renminbi* appreciation is not likely to shrink the trade balance.[158]

Rather, they argue that China's industrial policy is supported by other, more troubling "market-distorting tactics."[159]

At the top of this list are demands that U.S. and other foreign firms provide technology in exchange for Chinese market access.[160] According to a member of the delegation, "The Chinese government is more than happy to keep the focus on the currency because it's not the real problem."[161]

IMPORTS

Imports from China into the United States have risen from $100 billion in 2000 to $399 billion 2011. The top import categories have stayed fairly constant from 2000 to 2011: computer and electronic products, miscellaneous manufactured commodities, apparel, electrical equipment, leather goods, machinery and fabricated metal products. These are all manufacturing categories that gain competitive advantage from low labor prices in China.

In the past, Chinese exports to the United States have traditionally been low-value, labor intensive products such as toys and games, footwear, textiles and apparel. However, since China entered the WTO, an increasing proportion of U.S. imports from China have been comprised of more technologically advanced products.[162] Reflecting this trend, by far the largest growth sector in Chinese exports to the U.S. market has been computer and electronic products, increasing nearly six-fold from around $24.7 billion in 2000 to nearly $145.8 billion in 2011 (see Figure 19).

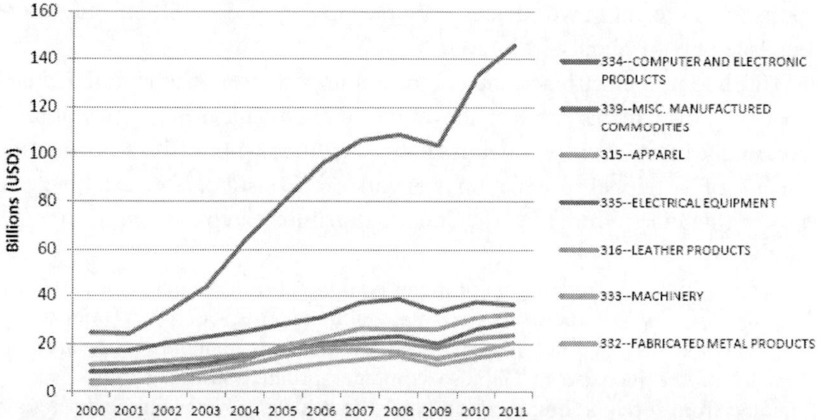

Figure 19. Imports (Top Imports), China to U.S. (2000-2011, NAIC, 3-digit).

Looking at the top Chinese exports to the United States for the period from 2000 to 2010 (see Appendix 2), the placement and variety of technologically advanced products has increased significantly. The top category of Chinese imports to the United States between 2000 and 2011 has consistently been automatic data processing machines (a category that includes computers). However, the #2 import category in 2011, electric apparatus for line telephony (a category that includes telephones, video phones and fax machines) was the #9 import category in 2000. The #3 import category in 2011, television receivers (including video monitors), was not a top 10 import in 2000. The #4 import category in 2011, toys (including video games), was also not on the list of top 10 imports in 2000. The #6 import in 2011, printers, again was not on the list of top 10 import categories in 2000. Note that while these items are classified as technologically advanced products for purposes of trade data, they are still by and large relatively low-tech consumer electronics.

Computers and Electronics

A portion of this growth may merely be the reallocation of computer and electronics imports from other parts of Asia to China. Comparing imports of computer and electronic products from China into the United States against imports of computer and electronic products from both Asia and the World from 2000 to 2011 (see Figure 22), exports from China have risen by around $121 billion (from $25 billion in 2000 to $145.8 billion in 2011), while exports from the entire world have only risen by about $92 billion and exports from Asia only by about $74 billion.

This boom in electronics and computers imports from China to the United States may also in part reflect the trends of non-Chinese manufacturers to increasingly locate their product assembly facilities within China, as the final segment of a global production network.[163] Consider, for example, the following statement from a recent Congressional Research Service report:

> [W]hile U.S. imports of computer equipment from China from 2000-2009 rose by 440 percent, the total value of U.S. computer imports worldwide rose by only 14 percent. Many analysts contend that a large share of the increase in Chinese computer production and exports has come from foreign computer companies that have moved manufacturing facilities to China. For example, Taiwan, one of the world's leaders in sales of information technology, produces over 90 percent of its information hardware equipment (such as computers) in China.[164]

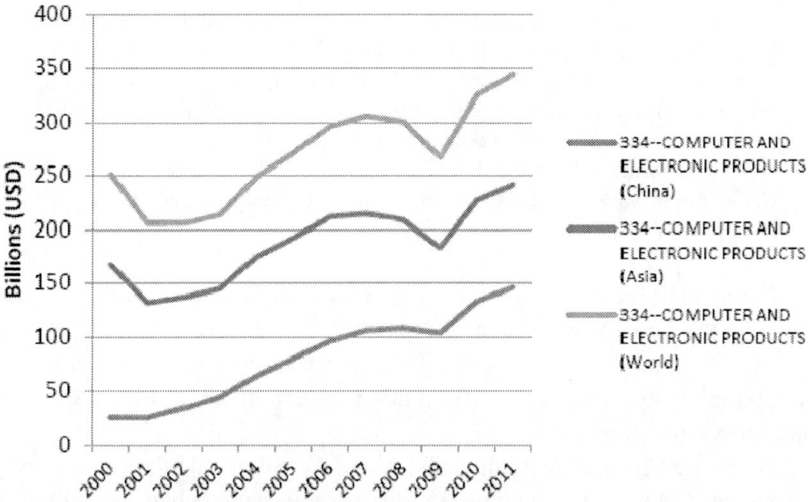

Figure 20. Imports (Computers and Electronics), World, Asia and China to U.S. (2000-2011, NAICS 3-digit).

Many Taiwanese companies have shifted production to China. In addition to well-known Hai Precision Industry – producer of products like Apple's iPad and Motorola cell phones – this includes companies like laptop computer producers Quanta Computer, Compal Electronics, Wistron, and Inventec Technology. These companies serve as contract designers and manufacturers for such non-Chinese brands as Hewlett-Packard, Dell and Acer. [165] That is to say, the increase in electronics and computer imports from China from 2000 to 2011 is not necessarily indicative of any newfound dominance in these categories by Chinese corporations or Chinese brands.

According to economist Sylvain Plasschaert, "a major part (around 60 percent of the exports out of China) is operated by 'foreign-invested enterprises'. This concept comprises both joint ventures between Chinese and foreign companies, and fully-owned affiliates of foreign enterprises as well. In other words, the label 'Made in China' is not synonymous with 'made by Chinese firms proper'."[166] The percentage of electronics and computer production operated by "foreign-invested enterprises" in China is likely even higher than this 60 percent. [167] As Dr. Theodore Moran noted in written testimony before the U.S.-China Economic and Security Review Commission on March 30, 2011:

> Foreign manufacturing investors have been responsible for more than 92 percent of all Chinese ATP [Advanced Technology Products] exports since 1996, and 96 percent since 2002. And within this 96 percent foreign investor-dominated channel, there has been a shift to wholly-owned MNC exporters from joint venture companies.
>
> State-owned Chinese enterprises have an ATP trade deficit with the US, while private Chinese firms and collective enterprises contribute very little to ATP trade.[168]

If the massive increase in imports of electronics and computers from China to the United States over the past decade is reflective of imports by MNCs (whose products are sourced globally but assembled in China), this has strong implications for the gains from these imports by both Chinese firms and the Chinese government.[169]

For many Chinese electronic and computer imports into the United States, the actual Chinese contribution to the overall value chain is quite low (essentially only the added value from assembly), even though the entire value of such imports into the United States are then attributed to China. According to Dr. Moran:

> The share of domestic value-added FDI operation in China in high skill-intensive sectors such as computers and telecommunications ranges from less than one-half to slightly more than one-half of what is found in other developing countries where comparable measures can be made, such as Mexico... the production of increasingly sophisticated goods destined for international markets from China has been remarkably well constrained to and contained within the plants owned and controlled by foreign multinationals and their international suppliers.[170]
>
> At the end of the day, China's high tech export explosion represents multinational corporations bringing high skill-content high value-added inputs into China, assembling them into final products (or semi-assembled intermediaries), and exporting them to world markets.[171]

Based upon the limited value added by Chinese firms in Chinese high-tech exports, Alyson C. Ma and Ari Van Assche have argued that, "once China's role in global production networks is taken into account, there is little evidence that China is rapidly moving up the technology ladder and becoming competitive in technology-intensive areas...

Rather, China's production activities have remained consistent with its comparative advantage in labor-intensive production activities."[172]

Outsourcing: "Win-Win" or Hollowing Out the U.S. Manufacturing Sector?

If U.S. corporations are manufacturing computers and electronics via networks of global (largely Asian) supply chains and then repatriating a large share of profits, this should *prima facie* benefit both U.S. companies and consumers and be a "win-win" situation. According to Wayne Morrison of the Congressional Research Service, "U.S. imports of low-cost goods from China greatly benefit U.S. consumers by increasing their purchasing power. U.S. firms that use China as the final point of assembly for their products, or use Chinese-made inputs for production in the United States, are able to lower costs and become more globally competitive."[173]

Becoming more globally competitive allows these firms to increase profits and/or market share, and should facilitate the hiring of more employees, both in the U.S. and abroad. Daniel J. Ikenson of the Cato Institute illustrates the potential for high-wage job creation in the United States by outsourcing low-value assembly tasks to China as follows:

> According to a widely cited 2007 study by Greg Linden, Kenneth L. Kraemer and Jason Dedrick of the University of California, Irvine, each Apple iPod costs $150 to produce. But only about $4 of that cost is Chinese value-added. Most of the value comes from components made in other countries, including the U.S. Yet when those iPods are imported from China, where they are snapped together, the full $150 is counted as an import from China... In reality, those imported iPods support thousands of U.S. jobs up the value chain — in engineering, design, finance, manufacturing, marketing, distribution, retail and elsewhere."[174]

The 2007 study by Greg Linden, *et al* seems to confirm Ikenson's claim:

> To summarize, the iPod supports nearly twice as many [mainly production] jobs offshore as in the U.S., yet wages paid in the U.S. are over twice as much as those paid overseas. Apple keeps most of its R&D, marketing, top management and corporate support functions in the U.S., creating over 5,800 professional and engineering jobs that can be attributed to the success of the iPod. The iPod also supports thousands of U.S. non-professional jobs, mostly in retail...[175]

However, some analysts warn that even this scenario – in which only low-value tasks are outsourced to China and high-value tasks are kept in the United States and other parts of Asia, such as Japan – could have a negative long-term impact upon the U.S. economy, based on the fact that large-scale outsourcing of manufacturing activities might lead to a hollowing out of America's industrial base. According to Greg Linden's report:

> As recently as 2000, over one-third of the jobs in the U.S. computer industry were production jobs. By 2007, the number of production workers had fall to less than one sixth of total employment, and total production jobs had been cut in half just since 2002.[176]

This means that American workers are losing basic skills. As Clyde Prestowitz writes:

> Over the past ten years there has been a massive loss of 8 million manufacturing jobs [in America]. That has been accompanied by substantial job creation in the services industries, but the bulk of the new jobs are in retailing and food service, which pay far less with far fewer benefits than manufacturing... China's workers today are not on average as well educated as U.S. workers. But the jobs are moving to China because the corporations can up-skill them on the line and make them highly productive. By the same token, just because the jobs are moving to China or elsewhere, American workers are to a certain extent being down-skilled as they move to more menial work in retailing or food service.[177]

Moreover, there is no guarantee that future job losses will be limited to low-wage production positions. Linden's report warns:

> Many U.S. high-tech companies are [already] investing in white-collar job creation offshore to tap pools of low-cost talent and gain access to growing markets... What is not known is whether innovative U.S. companies will continue to keep white-collar jobs in the U.S. while outsourcing production overseas... if globalization leads to a hollowing out of professional jobs as well as manufacturing, then innovation will only benefit shareholders, consumers, and a small number of top managers and professionals in the U.S.[178]

In addition to human resources, the large scale outsourcing of consumer electronics has also cost America associated infrastructure and a base of suppliers. According to Gary Pisano of Harvard Business School, this means that even if wages in China explode in the future, the shift in operations to low-wage countries like China has already become "almost irreversible."[179]

However, according to Andy Grove, chief executive officer or chairman at Intel from 1987 to 2005, the biggest danger of electronics outsourcing to China is to future innovation. As the "scaling process" (the process by which "technology goes from prototype to mass production") has moved to China, it has future breakthroughs with it. Mr. Grove illustrates the danger of breaking "the chain of experience that is so important in technological evolution" with the example of advanced batteries,

> It has taken years and many false starts, but finally we are about to witness mass- produced electric cars and trucks. They all rely on lithium-ion batteries... [and] the U.S. share of lithium-ion battery production is tiny... The U.S. lost its lead in batteries 30 years ago when it stopped making consumer electronic devices. Whoever made batteries then gained the exposure and relationships needed to learn to supply batteries for the more demanding laptop PC market, and after that, for the even more demanding automobile market. U.S. companies did not participate in the first phase and consequently were not in the running for all that followed. I doubt they will ever catch up."[180]

Solely considering computers and electronics exports from China to the United States presents a skewed understanding of the overall nature of exports from China to the United States from 2000 to 2011. Although computers and electronic products have seen significantly faster growth than any other category from 2000 to 2011, all of the top Chinese export categories have grown during this period. This includes many lower-tech products for which the share of Chinese value-added is considerably higher. (See Figure 21) The total value of computers and electronics exports from China to the United States amounted to more than $950 billion from 2000 to 2011, but all other exports from 2000 to 2011 amounted to more than $1.9 trillion. Thus, even if the case of the iPod is not an outlier and computer and electronic products only reflect a very low level of value-added in China, most of the exports from

China to the United States during this period still consisted of lower tech products that embody a higher level of value added in China (see Figure 21).

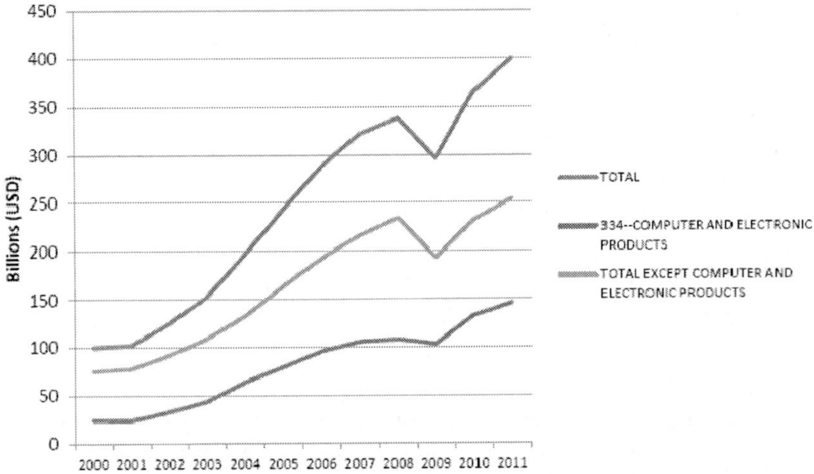

Figure 21. Imports (Computers and Electronics vs. Other), China to U.S. (2000-2011, NAICS 3-digit).

Demographic Trends and Their Potential Impact on Future Trade Patterns

While there are concerns in the United States over the size of the bilateral trade deficit with China, there are concerns in China that it cannot continue to grow indefinitely relying upon a model where it is simply the world's workshop. In the short- to medium-term, rising real wages in China,[181] coupled with the specters of inflation and regional labor shortages,[182] threaten to make China a less competitive export economy. While rising labor costs are not anticipated to affect decisions by computers and electronics firms — which are more heavily reliant upon investment in infrastructure and specialized skill sets[183] — for low-value, labor-intensive products higher wages will likely either translate into higher prices for consumers in the United States or into fewer orders for Chinese firms.[184] This trend has already begun to affect the manufacturing decisions of producers of textile goods and footwear, like Coach[185] and Payless Shoes.[186] Such firms may have to increasingly turn to countries other than China to supply them with cheap labor.

In the long-term, a rapidly aging population and the effects of China's "one child" policy are likely to exacerbate pressures upon China's low-income labor market. Whereas China's working age population (age 15 to 64) accounted for over 71 percent of China's total population in 2010,[187] this number is likely to drop in coming years.

Most importantly from the perspective of low-wage labor, there will be a "precipitous drop" in workers in their 20s. According to Feng Wang of the Brookings-Tsinghua Center,

> [B]etween 2016 and 2026, the size of the population in this age range will be reduced by about one-quarter, to 150 million from 200 million. For Chinese aged 20 to 24, that decline will come sooner and will be more drastic: Over the next decade, their number will be reduced by nearly 50 percent, to 68 million from 125 million. Such a drastic decline in the young labor force will usher in, for the first time in recent Chinese history, successive shrinking cohorts of labor force entrants... as a result of China's very low fertility over the past two decades, the abundance of young, inexpensive labor is soon to be history...[188]

As a result, according to Jianmin Li of The Jamestown Foundation, "The comparative advantage of cheap labor, on which China's economic growth and international competitive power rely on, will gradually be weakened or even lost, severely straining the vigor of economic development.

Under these circumstances, the traditional labor-intensive industries will face enormous pressure."[189]

Loss of competitiveness in labor-intensive, low-margin exports means that high-technology products will likely continue making up an increasing share of Chinese imports to the United States.

Perhaps in part because of the increasing difficulty of operating primarily as an export-based assembly hub, China has been looking to expand into higher value added exports of products made using Chinese-owned technology rather than continuing to just add a small portion of the value of high-tech products through assembly.

As the U.S. International Trade Commission puts it, "In a nutshell, China would like to shift from 'made in China' to 'created in China.'"[190]

The Trade Deficit in Advanced Technology Products (ATP)

Chinese advanced technology products (ATPs) are defined by the U.S. Census Bureau as high-technology products, encompassing a range from biotechnology and information and communications to aerospace, weapons, and nuclear technology.[191] U.S. ATP exports to China have steadily grown over the last decade, contributing to a widening trade imbalance. As Figure 24 shows, the main concentration of the ATPs imported from China in the last decade were information and communication products (comprising computers and computer parts, televisions, telephones, cameras, and monitors).[192] As the USCC's 2010 Annual Report noted, the U.S.-China ATP trade deficit has continued to expand in recent years, reaching $109 billion in 2011.[193]

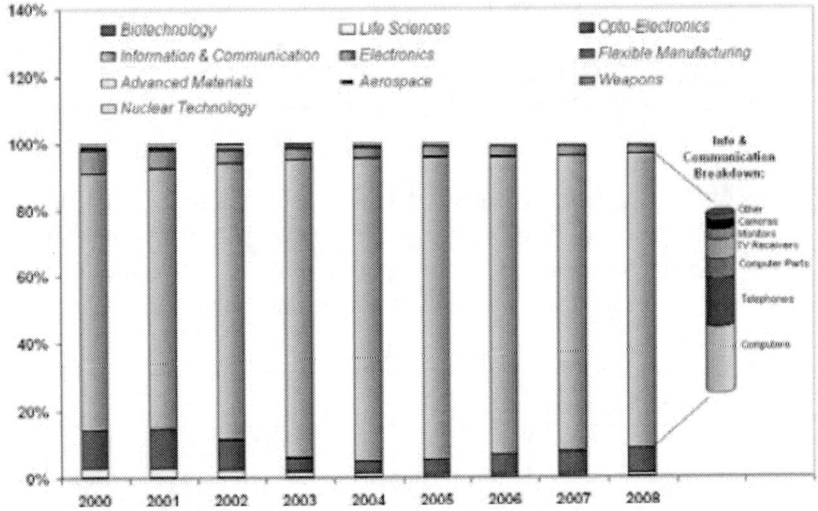

Source: World Trade Atlas.

Figure 22. U.S. ATP Imports from China (2000 – 2008).

Some analysts have pointed out, however, that a widening U.S. ATP trade deficit does not necessarily indicate Chinese dominance. There is great variety and use of ATPs, with the majority of Chinese exports to the U.S. being classified in the lower-tech information and communication category, while U.S. ATPs exports to China include semiconductors and more high-tech products.[194] Figure 23 shows that U.S. exports to China mainly consist of nuclear technology, information and communication, aerospace, and advanced materials.[195] Hence, the trade imbalance notwithstanding, there is still a sizeable gap in technology and quality between U.S. and Chinese ATP exports.

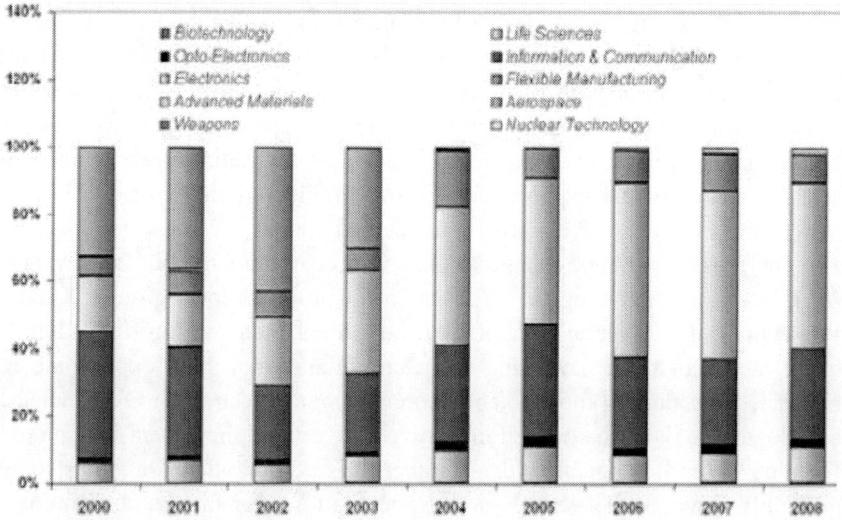

Source: World Trade Atlas.

Figure 23. U.S. ATP Exports to China (2000 – 2008).

Conclusion

Although U.S. exports to China have increased substantially since China entered the WTO in 2001, the overall value of these exports has failed to keep pace with the concurrent surge in imports from China. This has resulted in a huge and growing trade deficit between the United States and the People's Republic of China. The most obvious change in U.S. exports to China in 2011 versus 2000 is the dramatic rise in levels of non-manufactured goods. This includes both agricultural products to feed China's increasingly affluent and urbanizing population, and raw materials to feed China's growing industrial needs.[196] Whereas in 2000 the United States had a trade deficit with China in non-manufactured goods of around $283 million, by 2011 that had become a trade surplus of nearly $19.7 billion.

While the total value of manufactured exports from the United States to China rose more than six-fold from 2000 to 2011, much of this growth came in the form of intermediate goods rather than final goods: For example, computer components (like semi-conductors) rather than notebook computers, and basic chemicals (such as plastics used to make bags for packaging) rather than pharmaceuticals. The most notable exception to this pattern has been found in transportation equipment – primarily airplanes and automobiles — where, at least for the short- to medium- term, U.S. exports to China should remain strong. Sales of these sorts of transportation equipment may reflect a demand in China for higher tech items that China does not produce itself.[197] Possibly also reflecting this disparity in technological sophistication, there remains a "sizable technological gap between Chinese ATP imports [from the United States] and Chinese ATP exports [to the United States]."[198]

The most prominent change in U.S. imports from China in 2010 versus 2011 is a steady move up the value chain for products coming out of China. While the bulk of China's exports to the United States still reflect China's lower labor costs, an increasing share and quantity of these exports are in higher tech products – most notably, computers and electronics. Over the past decade, this may not have been indicative of a general movement by Chinese firms up the technological ladder— rather, it is possible that China has come to mainly serve as an assembly and export platform for foreign corporations, which took components manufactured elsewhere in world and put them together in China. Most recently, national champions like Lenovo, Huawei and Haier have begun to buck this trend, producing and exporting computers and consumer electronics with both high-value added in China and Chinese brand names. If China's efforts to spark "indigenous innovation" are successful (as it appears they already might be in green energy technologies[199], where Chinese companies have recently emerged as global leaders in wind[200] and solar power[201]), such national champions may be a sign of serious changes to come in the U.S.-China trade relationship.

The move "down" the value chain observed in U.S. exports to China, and the concurrent move "up" the value chain seen in Chinese exports to the United States, is connected. As more and more U.S. low- and medium-skill manufacturing has relocated overseas over the past decade – much, but not all of it to China – Chinese manufacturers (or at least, manufacturing facilities located in China) have absorbed a large portion of the former productive capacity of U.S. industry. U.S. manufacturers continue to maintain a competitive position in many higher-technology products, but whether or not the United States can maintain this technological edge will rely greatly on future market trends, as well as U.S. and Chinese trade policies.

APPENDIX 1: LIST OF TOP 10 EXPORTS FROM U.S. TO CHINA (HS, 4-DIGIT)

	2000	2001	2002	2003	2004
1	8802--AIRCRAFT, POWERED; SPACECRAFT & LAUNCH VEHICLES	8802--AIRCRAFT, POWERED; SPACECRAFT & LAUNCH VEHICLES	8802--AIRCRAFT, POWERED; SPACECRAFT & LAUNCH VEHICLES	1201--SOYBEANS, WHETHER OR NOT BROKEN	8542--ELECTRONIC INTEGRATED CIRCUITS & MICROASSEMBL, PTS
2	1201--SOYBEANS, WHETHER OR NOT BROKEN	1201--SOYBEANS, WHETHER OR NOT BROKEN	8542-- ELECTRONIC INTEGRATED CIRCUITS & MICROASSEMBL, PTS	8542-- ELECTRONIC INTEGRATED CIRCUITS & MICROASSEMBL, PTS	1201--SOYBEANS, WHETHER OR NOT BROKEN
3	8471--AUTOMATIC DATA PROCESS MACHINES; MAGN READER ETC 202	8471--AUTOMATIC DATA PROCESS MACHINES; MAGN READER ETC	1201--SOYBEANS, WHETHER OR NOT BROKEN	8802--AIRCRAFT, POWERED; SPACECRAFT & LAUNCH VEHICLES	8800 - CIVILIAN AIRCRAFT, ENGINES, AND PARTS
4	8542-- ELECTRONIC INTEGRATED CIRCUITS & MICROASSEMBL, PTS	8542-- ELECTRONIC INTEGRATED CIRCUITS & MICROASSEMBL, PTS	8471--AUTOMATIC DATA PROCESS MACHINES; MAGN READER ETC	5201--COTTON, NOT CARDED OR COMBED	5201--COTTON, NOT CARDED OR COMBED
5	3100-- FERTILIZERS, EXPORTS ONLY INCL OTHER CRUDE MAT'LS	8473--PARTS ETC FOR TYPEWRITERS & OTHER OFFICE MACHINES	3100-- FERTILIZERS, EXPORTS ONLY INCL OTHER CRUDE MAT'LS	8471--AUTOMATIC DATA PROCESS MACHINES; MAGN READER ETC	7204--FERROUS WASTE & SCRAP; REMELT SCR IRON/STEEL INGOT

(Continued)

	2000	2001	2002	2003	2004
6	8473--PARTS ETC FOR TYPEWRITERS & OTHER OFFICE MACHINES	8517--ELECTRIC APPARATUS FOR LINE TELEPHONY ETC, PARTS	8517--ELECTRIC APPARATUS FOR LINE TELEPHONY ETC, PARTS	7204--FERROUS WASTE & SCRAP; REMELT SCR IRON/STEEL INGOT	8471--AUTOMATIC DATA PROCESS MACHINES; MAGN READER ETC
7	8517--ELECTRIC APPARATUS FOR LINE TELEPHONY ETC, PARTS	3100--FERTILIZERS, EXPORTS ONLY INCL OTHER CRUDE MAT'LS	7204--FERROUS WASTE & SCRAP; REMELT SCR IRON/STEEL INGOT	8473--PARTS ETC FOR TYPEWRITERS & OTHER OFFICE MACHINES	8479--MACHINES ETC HAVING INDIVIDUAL FUNCTIONS
8	8479--MACHINES ETC HAVING INDIVIDUAL FUNCTIONS NESOI, PT	7204--FERROUS WASTE & SCRAP; REMELT SCR IRON/STEEL INGOT	8473--PARTS ETC FOR TYPEWRITERS & OTHER OFFICE MACHINES	3100--FERTILIZERS, EXPORTS ONLY INCL OTHER CRUDE MAT'LS	8473--PARTS ETC FOR TYPEWRITERS & OTHER OFFICE MACHINES
9	4101--RAW HIDES & SKINS OF BOVINE OR EQUINE ANIMALS	4101--RAW HIDES & SKINS OF BOVINE OR EQUINE ANIMALS	8479--MACHINES ETC HAVING INDIVIDUAL FUNCTIONS	7404--COPPER WASTE AND SCRAP	7404--COPPER WASTE AND SCRAP
10	8803--PARTS OF AIRCRAFT, SPACECRAFT ETC	8479--MACHINES ETC HAVING INDIVIDUAL FUNCTIONS	4101--RAW HIDES & SKINS OF BOVINE OR EQUINE ANIMALS	8517--ELECTRIC APPARATUS FOR LINE TELEPHONY ETC, PARTS	8517--ELECTRIC APPARATUS FOR LINE TELEPHONY ETC, PARTS

Year by Year – Top 10 Exports (2005 to 2009) (HS, 4-digits)

	2005	2006	2007	2008	2009
1	8800 - CIVILIAN AIRCRAFT, ENGINES, AND PARTS	8542--ELECTRONIC INTEGRATED CIRCUITS & MICROASSEMBL, PTS	8542--ELECTRONIC INTEGRATED CIRCUITS & MICROASSEMBL, PTS	1201--SOYBEANS, WHETHER OR NOT BROKEN	1201--SOYBEANS, WHETHER OR NOT BROKEN
2	8542--ELECTRONIC INTEGRATED CIRCUITS & MICROASSEMBL, PTS	8800 - CIVILIAN AIRCRAFT, ENGINES, AND PARTS	8800 - CIVILIAN AIRCRAFT, ENGINES, AND PARTS	8542--ELECTRONIC INTEGRATED CIRCUITS & MICROASSEMBL, PTS	8800 - CIVILIAN AIRCRAFT, ENGINES, AND PARTS
3	1201--SOYBEANS, WHETHER OR NOT BROKEN	1201--SOYBEANS, WHETHER OR NOT BROKEN	1201--SOYBEANS, WHETHER OR NOT BROKEN	8800 - CIVILIAN AIRCRAFT, ENGINES, AND PARTS	8542--ELECTRONIC INTEGRATED CIRCUITS & MICROASSEMBL, PTS
4	5201--COTTON, NOT CARDED OR COMBED	5201--COTTON, NOT CARDED OR COMBED	7204--FERROUS WASTE & SCRAP; REMELT SCR IRON/STEEL INGOT	7204--FERROUS WASTE & SCRAP; REMELT SCR IRON/STEEL INGOT	7204--FERROUS WASTE & SCRAP; REMELT SCR IRON/STEEL INGOT
5	7204--FERROUS WASTE & SCRAP; REMELT SCR IRON/STEEL INGOT	7204--FERROUS WASTE & SCRAP; REMELT SCR IRON/STEEL INGOT	7404--COPPER WASTE AND SCRAP	7404--COPPER WASTE AND SCRAP	--WASTE AND SCRAP OF PAPER OR PAPERBOARD
6	8473--PARTS ETC FOR TYPEWRITERS & OTHER OFFICE MACHINES	7404--COPPER WASTE AND SCRAP	7602--ALUMINUM WASTE AND SCRAP	7602--ALUMINUM WASTE AND SCRAP	7404--COPPER WASTE AND SCRAP

(Continued)

	2005	2006	2007	2008	2009
7	8471--AUTOMATIC DATA PROCESS MACHINES; MAGN READER ETC	7602--ALUMINUM WASTE AND SCRAP	4707--WASTE AND SCRAP OF PAPER OR PAPERBOARD	5201--COTTON, NOT CARDED OR COMBED	7602--ALUMINUM WASTE AND SCRAP
8	7602--ALUMINUM WASTE AND SCRAP	8473--PARTS ETC FOR TYPEWRITERS & OTHER OFFICE MACHINES	5201--COTTON, NOT CARDED OR COMBED	4707--WASTE AND SCRAP OF PAPER OR PAPERBOARD	8517--ELECTRIC APPARATUS FOR LINE TELEPHONY ETC, PARTS
9	7404--COPPER WASTE AND SCRAP	4707--WASTE AND SCRAP OF PAPER OR PAPERBOARD	8473--PARTS ETC FOR TYPEWRITERS & OTHER OFFICE MACHINES	8517--ELECTRIC APPARATUS FOR LINE TELEPHONY ETC, PARTS	3901--POLYMERS OF ETHYLENE, IN PRIMARY FORMS
10	4707--WASTE AND SCRAP OF PAPER OR PAPERBOARD	8471--AUTOMATIC DATA PROCESS MACHINES; MAGN READER ETC	8486--MACH/APPS FOR MANUFCT OF SEMICNDCT BOULES,ETC, PART	8703--MOTOR CARS & VEHICLES FOR TRANSPORTING PERSONS	8703--MOTOR CARS & VEHICLES FOR TRANSPORTING PERSONS

Top Exports (2010)

1. 1201--SOYBEANS, WHETHER OR NOT BROKEN
2. 8800 - CIVILIAN AIRCRAFT, ENGINES, AND PARTS CIVILIAN AIRCRAFT, ENGINES, AND PARTS
3. 8542--ELECTRONIC INTEGRATED CIRCUITS & MICROASSEMBL, PTS
4. 8703--MOTOR CARS & VEHICLES FOR TRANSPORTING PERSONS
5. 7404--COPPER WASTE AND SCRAP
6. 5201--COTTON, NOT CARDED OR COMBED
7. 7602--ALUMINUM WASTE AND SCRAP
8. 7204--FERROUS WASTE & SCRAP; REMELT SCR IRON/STEEL INGOT
9. 4707--WASTE AND SCRAP OF PAPER OR PAPERBOARD
10. 8486--MACH/APPS FOR MANUFCT OF SEMICNDCT BOULES,ETC,PART

APPENDIX 2. LIST OF TOP 10 IMPORTS FROM U.S. TO CHINA (HS, 4-DIGIT)

	2000	2001	2002	2003	2004
1	8471--AUTOMATIC DATA PROCESS MACHINES[203]	8471--AUTOMATIC DATA PROCESS MACHINES	8471--AUTOMATIC DATA PROCESS MACHINES	8471--AUTOMATIC DATA PROCESS MACHINES	8471--AUTOMATIC DATA PROCESS MACHINES
2	9503--TOYS	9503--TOYS	9503--TOYS	9503--TOYS	8473--PARTS ETC FOR TYPEWRITERS & OTHER OFFICE MACHINES
3	6403--FOOTWEAR, OUTER SOLE RUB, PLAST OR LEA & UPPER LEA	6403--FOOTWEAR, OUTER SOLE RUB, PLAST OR LEA & UPPER LEA	6403--FOOTWEAR, OUTER SOLE RUB, PLAST OR LEA & UPPER LEA	6403--FOOTWEAR, OUTER SOLE RUB, PLAST OR LEA & UPPER LEA	8525--TRANS APPAR FOR RADIOTELE ETC; TV CAMERA & REC
4	8473--PARTS ETC FOR TYPEWRITERS & OTHER OFFICE MACHINES	8473--PARTS ETC FOR TYPEWRITERS & OTHER OFFICE MACHINES	8473--PARTS ETC FOR TYPEWRITERS & OTHER OFFICE MACHINES	8473--PARTS ETC FOR TYPEWRITERS & OTHER OFFICE MACHINES	6403--FOOTWEAR, OUTER SOLE RUB, PLAST OR LEA & UPPER LEA
5	6402--FOOTWEAR, OUTER SOLE & UPPER RUBBER OR PLAST	9403—FURNITURE	9403--FURNITURE	9403--FURNITURE	9503--TOYS
6	9405--LAMPS & LIGHTING FITTINGS & PARTS	6402--FOOTWEAR, OUTER SOLE & UPPER RUBBER OR PLAST	9405--LAMPS & LIGHTING FITTINGS & PARTS	8525--TRANS APPAR FOR RADIOTELE ETC; TV CAMERA & REC	9403--FURNITURE

(Continued)

7	8527--RECEPTION APPARATUS FOR RADIOTELEPHONY	9405--LAMPS & LIGHTING FITTINGS & PARTS	6402--FOOTWEAR, OUTER SOLE & UPPER RUBBER OR PLAST	9504--ARTICLES FOR ARCADE, TABLE OR PARLOR GAMES, PARTS	4202--TRAVEL GOODS, HANDBAGS, WALLETS, JEWELRY CASES ETC
8	9403--FURNITURE	8527--RECEPTION APPARATUS FOR RADIOTELEPHONY	8525--TRANS APPAR FOR RADIOTELE ETC; TV CAMERA & REC	4202—TRAVEL GOODS, HANDBAGS, WALLETS, JEWELRY CASES ETC	9504--ARTICLES FOR ARCADE, TABLE OR PARLOR GAMES, PARTS
9	8517—ELECTRIC APPARATUS FOR LINE TELEPHONY	4202--TRAVEL GOODS, HANDBAGS, WALLETS, JEWELRY CASES ETC	4202—TRAVEL GOODS, HANDBAGS, WALLETS, JEWELRY CASES ETC	9405--LAMPS & LIGHTING FITTINGS & PARTS	9401--SEATS (EXCEPT BARBER, DENTAL, ETC), AND PARTS
10	4202--TRAVEL GOODS, HANDBAGS, WALLETS, JEWELRY CASES ETC	8517--ELECTRIC APPARATUS FOR LINE TELEPHONY	9504--ARTICLES FOR ARCADE, TABLE OR PARLOR GAMES, PARTS	9401--SEATS (EXCEPT BARBER, DENTAL, ETC), AND PARTS	9405--LAMPS & LIGHTING FITTINGS & PARTS

	2005	2006	2007	2008	2009
1	8471--AUTOMATIC DATA PROCESS MACHINES	8471--AUTOMATIC DATA PROCESS MACHINES	8471--AUTOMATIC DATA PROCESS MACHINES	8471--AUTOMATIC DATA PROCESS MACHINES	8471--AUTOMATIC DATA PROCESS MACHINES
2	8525--TRANS APPAR FOR RADIOTELE ETC; TV CAMERA & REC	8525--TRANS APPAR FOR RADIOTELE ETC; TV CAMERA & REC	8517--ELECTRIC APPARATUS FOR LINE TELEPHONY	8517--ELECTRIC APPARATUS FOR LINE TELEPHONY	8517--ELECTRIC APPARATUS FOR LINE TELEPHONY

	2005	2006	2007	2008	2009
3	8473--PARTS ETC FOR TYPEWRITERS & OTHER OFFICE MACHINES	8473--PARTS ETC FOR TYPEWRITERS & OTHER OFFICE MACHINES	8528--TV RECVRS, INCL VIDEO MONITORS & PROJECTORS	8528--TV RECVRS, INCL VIDEO MONITORS & PROJECTORS	8528--TV RECVRS, INCL VIDEO MONITORS & PROJECTORS
4	6403--FOOTWEAR, OUTER SOLE RUB, PLAST OR LEA & UPPER LEA	9403--FURNITURE	9504—ARTICLES FOR ARCADE, TABLE OR PARLOR GAMES, PARTS	9504—ARTICLES FOR ARCADE, TABLE OR PARLOR GAMES, PARTS	9504--ARTICLES FOR ARCADE, TABLE OR PARLOR GAMES, PARTS
5	9503--TOYS	6403--FOOTWEAR, OUTER SOLE RUB, PLAST OR LEA & UPPER LEA	8473--PARTS ETC FOR TYPEWRITERS & OTHER OFFICE MACHINES	8473--PARTS ETC FOR TYPEWRITERS & OTHER OFFICE MACHINES	9503--TOYS
6	9403--FURNITURE	8528--TV RECVRS, INCL VIDEO MONITORS & PROJECTORS	9503--TOYS	9503--TOYS	8473--PARTS ETC FOR TYPEWRITERS & OTHER OFFICE MACHINES
7	8528--TV RECVRS, INCL VIDEO MONITORS & PROJECTORS	9503--TOYS	9403--FURNITURE	9403--FURNITURE	6403--FOOTWEAR, OUTER SOLE RUB, PLAST OR LEA & UPPER LEA
8	9504--ARTICLES FOR ARCADE, TABLE OR PARLOR GAMES, PARTS	9504--ARTICLES FOR ARCADE, TABLE OR PARLOR GAMES, PARTS	8443--PRINT MACH INCL INK-JET MACH ANCIL T PRNT PT	6403--FOOTWEAR, OUTER SOLE RUB, PLAST OR LEA & UPPER LEA	8443--PRINT MACH INCL INK-JET MACH ANCIL T PRNT PT

(Continued)

	2005	2006	2007	2008	2009
9	9401--SEATS (EXCEPT BARBER, DENTAL, ETC), AND PARTS	9401--SEATS (EXCEPT BARBER, DENTAL, ETC), AND PARTS	6403--FOOTWEAR, OUTER SOLE RUB, PLAST OR LEA & UPPER LEA	8443--PRINT MACH INCL INK-JET MACH ANCIL T PRNT PT	9403--FURNITURE
10	4202--TRAVEL GOODS, HANDBAGS, WALLETS, JEWELRY CASES ETC	4202--TRAVEL GOODS, HANDBAGS, WALLETS, JEWELRY CASES ETC	9401--SEATS (EXCEPT BARBER, DENTAL, ETC), AND PARTS	9401--SEATS (EXCEPT BARBER, DENTAL, ETC), AND PARTS	9401--SEATS (EXCEPT BARBER, DENTAL, ETC), AND PARTS

Top Imports (2010)

1. 8471--AUTOMATIC DATA PROCESS MACHINES; MAGN READER ETC
2. 8517--ELECTRIC APPARATUS FOR LINE TELEPHONY ETC, PARTS
3. 8528--TV RECVRS, INCL VIDEO MONITORS & PROJECTORS
4. 8473--PARTS ETC FOR TYPEWRITERS & OTHER OFFICE MACHINES
5. 9503--TOYS NESOI; SCALE MODELS ETC; PUZZLES; PARTS ETC
6. 9504--ARTICLES FOR ARCADE, TABLE OR PARLOR GAMES, PARTS
7. 8443--PRINT MACH INCL INK-JET MACH ANCIL T PRNT PT NESOI
8. 6403--FOOTWEAR, OUTER SOLE RUB, PLAST OR LEA & UPPER LEA
9. 9403--FURNITURE NESOI AND PARTS THEREOF
10. 9401--SEATS (EXCEPT BARBER, DENTAL, ETC), AND PARTS

End Notes

[1] United States International Trade Commission, “Shifts in U.S. Merchandise Trade 2010,” Publication No. 4245, August 2011, p. 3-5.

[2] United States International Trade Commission, “Shifts in U.S. Merchandise Trade 2009,” Publication No. 4179, August 2010, p. 3-5.

[3] United States International Trade Commission, “Shifts in U.S. Merchandise Trade 2010,” Publication No. 4245, August 2011, p. 8-9.

[4] Office of the United States Trade Representative, “Background Information on China's Accession to the World Trade Organization”, December 11 2011, http://ustraderep.gov/

[5] Wayne Morrison, *China-U.S. Trade Issues*, Congressional Research Service, Washington, DC, January 2011, p. 16.

[6] “China lifted long-standing bans on the importation of agricultural goods such as corn, wheat, citrus products and meat (during the course of the U.S.-China bilateral negotiations as a sign of good faith). China must implement tariff-rate quotas that provide significant market access for bulk goods of special importance to American farmers such as grains, soy oil and cotton upon accession. China has agreed to eliminate import monopolies maintained by State trading enterprises on agricultural goods such as wheat, rice and corn and to permit non-State trading enterprises to import them.” (Office of the United States Trade Representative, “Background Information on China's Accession to the World Trade Organization”, December 11 2011, http://ustraderep.gov/)

[7] Washington File, *Transcript: Clinton March 29 Comments on U.S.-China Relations*, March 30, 2000, http://usinfo.org/wf-archive/2000/000330/epf401.htm

[8] Washington File, *Transcript: Clinton March 29 Comments on U.S.-China Relations*, March 30, 2000, http://usinfo.org/wf-archive/2000/000330/epf401.htm

[9] Doug Bandow, “Trade with China: Business Profits or Human Rights?”, Cato Institute, http://www.cato.org/pub display.php?pub id=4713

[10] This is not to say that there was no debate over economic issues. For example, “USCC Commissioner Pat Mulloy noted at the June 9[, 2010] hearing that one person had correctly analyzed the deal: Joseph Quinlan, an economist with Morgan Stanley. Quoted in the Wall Street Journal, Quinlan said: ‘While the debate in Washington focused mainly on the probable lift for U.S. exports to China, many U.S. multinationals have something different in mind. The deal is about investment, not exports.’” (Richard A. McCormack, “China's Entry Into The WTO 10 Years Later Is Not What President Clinton Promised”, *Manufacturing & Technology News*, June 15, 2010.)

[11] Unless otherwise specified, data for this report was generated using TradeStats Express from the U.S. Department of Commerce's Office of Trade Industry Information’s Trade Policy Information System (TPIS).

[12] Xinhua News, “China becomes 3rd largest export market of U.S. in 2007 ,” March 5, 2008. http://english.gov.cn/2008-03/05/content_909530.htm

[13] U.S.-China Business Council, "Top US Export Markets in 2011 ($ billion)," 2012. https://www.uschina.org/public/exports

[14] U.S.-China Business Council, "Top US Export Markets in 2011 ($ billion)," 2012. https://www.uschina.org/public/exports

[15] U.S.-China Business Council, “US Exports to China by State: 2000-2010”, 2011, http://www.uschina.org/

[16] Unless otherwise specified, all figures in this report are in nominal U.S. dollars.

[17] http://tse.export.gov. Moreover, these increased exports have not originated from a single source or industry. "Twenty-four states exported more than $1 billion to China in 2010." (U.S.-China Business Council, "US Exports to China by State: 2000-2010", 2011, http://www.uschina.org/).

[18] http://www.census.gov/foreign-trade

[19] Wayne Morrison, *China-U.S. Trade Issues*, Congressional Research Service, Washington, DC, January 2011, p. 5.

[20] Wayne Morrison, *China-U.S. Trade Issues*, Congressional Research Service, Washington, DC, January 2011, p. 6.

[21] Office of the United States Trade Representative, "US-China Trade Facts," 2012. http://www.ustr.gov/countriesregions/china

[22] This report looks at exports and imports in terms of dollar values. This must be made with two caveats. First, these dollar values are not adjusted for inflation or differences in the exchange rate between the U.S. and China. Second, the same value worth of soy beans or waste likely takes up more volume than that value worth of cars. For both these reasons, this report does not claim to reflect the changing composition of imports or exports in terms of volume traded, but rather only in terms of nominal dollar value.

[23] Wayne Morrison, "China-U.S. Trade Issues," Congressional Research Service, Washington, DC, September 30, 2011, p. 2.

[24] Michael F. Martin, "What's the Difference? – Comparing U.S. and Chinese Trade Data, *Congressional Research Service,* April 21, 2010.

[25] K.C. Fung, Lawrence J. Lau and Yangyan Xiong, "Adjusted Estimates of United States-China Bilateral Trade Balances — An Update" *Stanford Center for International Development*, Working Paper No. 278, June 2006.

[26] Dick K. Nanto and J. Michael Donnelly, "U.S. International Trade: Trends and Forecasts", *Congressional Research Service*, September 6, 2011.

[27] U.S.-China Economic and Security Review Commission, *2004 Report to Congress*, June 2004, p. 254.

[28] U.S.-China Economic and Security Review Commission, *2008 Report to Congress*, November 2008, p. 6.

[29] U.S.-China Economic and Security Review Commission, *2008 Report to Congress*, November 2008, pp. 85-86.

[30] Andrew Higgins, "From China, a run around U.S. tariffs", *Washington Post*, May 23, 2011.

[31] NAICS, 3-digit. "The North American Industry Classification System (NAICS) is the standard used by Federal statistical agencies in classifying business establishments for the purpose of collecting, analyzing, and publishing statistical data related to the U.S. business economy." (From U.S. Census Bureau, http://www.census.gov/)

[32] NAICS, 3-digit.

[33] NAICS. Generally, non-manufactured goods are goods which are in an unprocessed state (e.g. iron ore), whereas manufactured goods have been processed (e.g. televisions). While scrap and waste are derived from previously manufactured goods, they can be understood as non-manufactured goods in evaluating exports.

[34] NAICS, 2-digit

[35] NAICS 2122 and 2121.

[36] "Exports of U.S. agriculture products hit an all-time high in 2010. U.S. Agriculture Secretary Tom Vilsack says it's because U.S. producers are the best on Earth, resulting in high demand for U.S. products, especially on the far side of the Pacific. 'China became our number one market, surpassing Canada,' said Vilsack, in an interview provided by the

USDA. 'Ag exports to China were over $17.5 billion in the calendar year; that's up from $13.1 billion in calendar year 2009, a 34 percent increase.'" (Tom Steever, "China is number one U.S. ag customer", *Brownfield: Ag News for America*, February 12, 2011, http://brownfieldagnews.com/)

[37] Ben Baden, "From Cars to Soybeans, US Exports to China Are Booming," *China Business Review*, July-September 2012, https://www.chinabusinessreview.com/public /1207/baden. html

[38] "The Harmonized System or simply HS Code is the most widely used system for classifying traded goods. Every product traded is classified into a 10-digit code. The first two digits of the products code corresponds to one of the 98 HS "chapters," that classify all goods in general categories." (Michael Martin, "What's the Difference? – Comparing U.S. and Chinese Trade Data", Congressional Research Service, April 10, 2007, p.2.) HS category 8802 is used from 2000 to 2003 and HS category 8800 is used from 2004 to reflect exports of aircraft and parts.

[39] *The Economist*, "Business This Week", January 15 2011, p.7.

[40] Howard Schneider, "China food choices reshaping world markets", *The Washington Post*, May 23, 2011.

[41] *The Economist*, "Business This Week," January 15, 2011.

[42] Over two-thirds of cooking oil consumed in China comes from soybeans

[43] Whitney McFerron and Phoebe Sedgman, "Soybeans Top $17 for First Time on U.S. Exports Demand," Bloomberg Businessweek, August 21, 2012. http://www.businessweek.com/news /2012-08-21/soybeans for-first-time-as-demand-jumps-for-u-dot-s-dot-exports

[44] Whitney McFerron and Phoebe Sedgman, "Soybeans Top $17 for First Time on U.S. Exports Demand," Bloomberg Businessweek, August 21, 2012. http://www.businessweek.com/news /2012-08-21/soybeans for-first-time-as-demand-jumps-for-u-dot-s-dot-exports

[45] Clyde Russell, "China soybean import demand to wane, softening prices," Reuters, August 13, 2012. http://articles.chicagotribune.com/2012-08-13/news/sns-rt-us-column-russell-soy-chinabre87c069- 20120812_1_soybean-imports-tonnes

[46] Rodrigo Orihuela and Mario Sergio Lima, "Brazil Beating U.S. in Soybean Exports is Boon for All: Freight," *Bloomberg News*, Nov. 27, 2012. *http://www.bloomberg.com/news/2012-11-28/brazil-beating-u-s-in-soybeanexports-is-boon-for-all-freight.html.*

[47] Excerpted from Minnesota Soybean Research & Promotion Council, "Minnesota Benefits from $6.6 Billion Purchase of U.S. Soybeans by China", http://www.mnsoybean.org/

[48] "China will have more difficulty feeding itself in the coming years as expanding demand, spurred by increased urbanization, strains resources, Vice Minister of Agriculture Chen Xiaohua said. As more people move into cities and towns, the supply of farm products is limited by declining productivity of rural labor, a worsening natural environment and more extreme weather, Chen said in a transcript of a speech released by the department on Jan. 26." (William Bi, "China Faces More Difficulty Meeting Food Demand, Official Says", January 31, 2011, *Bloomberg News*.)

[49] "China wraps up record US soybean deal", *Reuters*, January 21, 2011.

[50] Excerpted from Minnesota Soybean Research & Promotion Council, "Minnesota Benefits from $6.6 Billion Purchase of U.S. Soybeans by China", http://www.mnsoybean.org/

[51] Jeff Wilson, "China to Buy $4.3 Billion of Soybeans in Deals With U.S. Exporters in Iowa," Bloomberg News. February 15, 2012. http://www.bloomberg.com/news/2012-02-15/china-to-buy-4-3-billion-of-soybeans-

[52] Jeff Wilson, "China to buy $4.3 billion of soybeans in deals with U.S. exporters in Iowa," Bloomberg, February 15, 2012.

[53] "China banned U.S. beef in December 2003 after the first case of bovine spongiform encephalopathy, or mad-cow disease, was discovered in the U.S. Back then, U.S. beef exports to China were relatively small--about $23 million... The potential market China represents now, though, is much larger and growing... Gregg Doud, chief economist for the U.S.-based National Cattlemen's Beef Association, said the Chinese beef market could be worth $200 million a year now to U.S. exporters if the ban was lifted." (*Meat Trade Daily News*, "China - Green light expected for US beef", June 27, 2010, http://www.meattradenewsdaily.co.uk/) Multiple factors now keep U.S. beef out of China. For example, "one beef-related issue limiting U.S. sales is the zero tolerance policies of China and Taiwan for beef that contains ractopamine, a feed additive that aims to raise leaner beef." (*Inside US-China Trade*, "Kirk Says Administration Seeks 'Immediate Progress' on Trade At S&ED", April 19, 2011.)

[54] According to their website, McHenry, Illinois-based Allendale, Inc. is "one of the largest commodity research advisory firms in the United States and one of the few remaining brokerage firms that develops its own economic research." (http://www.allendale-inc.com/about/whoweare.aspx)

[55] "Silence on beef imports during China President's visit in Washington", *Feedstuffs,* January 20, 2011, http://www.feedstuffs.com/

[56] HS, category 24.

[57] "Since 1886, Tobacco International has been the tobacco industry's leading trade journal." http://www.tobaccointernational.com/

[58] John Parker, "China's Leaf Tobacco Imports Show Upward Trend", Tobacco International, September 2007.

[59] According to The Foreign Trade Division of the U.S. Census Bureau, Unmanufactured tobacco made up over 99.9% percent of total tobacco exports in 2010 versus 34 percent in 2000. (http://tse.export.gov)

[60] Business Wire, "Research and Markets: Research Report on China's Cigarette Industry - 2010-2012", December 23, 2010, http://www.businesswire.com/.

[61] Keith Bradsher, "U.N. Food Agency Issues Warning on China Drought", *The New York Times*, February 8, 2011.

[62] Howard Schneider, "China food choices reshaping world markets", *The Washington Post*, May 23, 2011.

[63] HS 4-digit. From 2009 to 2011, the relative importance of two these waste categories declined (ferrous waste went from the 4th largest export to the 8th, and paper waste from the 5th to the 9th), aluminum waste and scrap rose from the 7th to the 6th largest export and copper waste and scrap went from the 6th to the 5th largest export. (See Appendix 1).

[64] The U.S. also exported a wide range of other types of waste and scrap to China in 2009, including plastic, rubber and various other types of metals. U.S. exports of other types of waste and scrap to China totaled over $489 million in 2009. This does not include reputed illegal exports of waste from the U.S. to China, like toxic e-waste. (For more information on e-waste see 60 Minutes, "Following the Trail Of Toxic E-Waste: 60 Minutes Follows America's Toxic Electronic Waste As It Is Illegally Shipped To Become China's Dirty Secret", August 30, 2009, http://www.cbsnews.com/)

[65] According to a *New York Times* article from 2004, "Much of the material being used to build China's skyscrapers, factories and telecommunications systems – along with many of the products it exports – is derived from scrap, which is usually cheaper than new metal made from ore." (Andrew Pollack and Keith Bradsher, "China's Need for Metal Keeps U.S. Scrap Dealers Scrounging", *The New York Times*, March 13, 2004.) According to some sources,

paper waste on the other hand may be "re-manufactured into cardboard to pack valuable manufactured goods for export back to the United States." (Richard McCormack, "U.S. Container Exports Still Dominated By Junk -- Scrap Paper, Scrap Metal and Bulk Commodities", *Manufacturing and Technology News*, July 31, 2008.)

[66] "Scrap dealers argue that in some cases, the scrap going to China would be of no use to Americans because it would cost too much to sort into its various parts. But withChina's cheap labor, that effort is affordable. 'We send everything to China,' said Danny C. Yiu, vice president of Ekco Metals... ''They will use chisels, hammers, hand tools to break this apart and sort it out.''' (Andrew Pollack and Keith Bradsher, "China's Need for Metal Keeps U.S. Scrap Dealers Scrounging", *The New York Times*, March 13, 2004.)

[67] From Andrew Pollack and Keith Bradsher, "China's Need for Metal Keeps U.S. Scrap Dealers Scrounging", The New York Times, March 13, 2004.

[68] Richard McCormack, "U.S. Container Exports Still Dominated By Junk -- Scrap Paper, Scrap Metal And Bulk Commodities", *Manufacturing and Technology News*, July 31, 2008.

[69] Clyde Prestowitz, "America Needs a New Globalization Game", *The Huffington Post,* April 29, 2010.

[70] China Daily, "Slowdown Hurts China's Scrap Metal Dealers", December 10, 2008.

[71] Copper and aluminum scrap exports fell from a combined $3.56 billion in 2008 to only a combined $2.62 billion in 2009.

[72] Dan Levin, "China's Big Recycling Market Is Sagging", *The New York Times*, March 11, 2009.

[73] In particular, computers & electronics declined from 26.1 percent of all U.S. exports to China in 2000 to around 16.6 percent in 2010.

[74] In 2010, amongst all manufactured goods, the U.S. also had an even smaller trade surplus with China in beverages & tobacco products (NAICS 312) and petroleum and coal products (NAICS 324).

[75] Paul Wiseman, "Despite China's might, US factories maintain edge", *Associated Press*, January 31, 2011.

[76] Nick Carey and James B. Kelleher, "Does corporate America kowtow to China", *Reuters*, April 27, 2011.

[77] Clyde Prestowitz, "Clyde Prestowitz: The Betrayal of American Prosperity (Excerpt)", May 11, 2010, http://www.progressivereader.com/?p=58997.

[78] Robert E. Scott, "Growing U.S. trade deficit with China cost 2.7 million jobs between 2001 and 2011," Economic Policy Institute, August 23, 2012. http://www.epi.org/publication /bp345-china-growing-trade-deficit

[79] Robert E. Scott, "Growing U.S. trade deficit with China cost 2.7 million jobs between 2001 and 2011," Economic Policy Institute, August 23, 2012. http://www.epi.org/publication /bp345-china-growing-trade-deficit

[80] Robert E. Scott, "Growing U.S. trade deficit with China cost 2.8 million jobs between 2001 and 2010", September 20, 2011, Economic Policy Institute, www.epi.org

[81] Daniel Ikenson, "China Trade and American Jobs", Cato Institute, April 2, 2010. http://www.cato.org/pub display.php?pub id=11652

[82] Trevor Williams, "The China Trade Deficit and U.S. Job Loss: Interview with an Economist", Global Atlanta, April 9, 2010, www.globalatlanta.com

[83] This is a joint product of Arizona State University and the Kearny Alliance, whose mission is "Aid through Trade".

[84] "Has China Really Stolen American Jobs?", http://www.futureofuschinatrade.com/article/us-china-tradeanalysis-has-china-really-stolen-american-jobs

[85] Fred Bergsten, "Beijing Is Key to Creating More U.S. Jobs", *Foreign Policy*, April 14, 2010.

[86] Computer equipment was the top subcategory and fell from 34.9 percent in 2000 to only 15.9 percent in 2009. Semiconductors and other electronic components rose from 31.3 percent in 2000 to 48.4 percent in 2009.

[87] Alexander Hammer, Robert Koopman and Andrew Martinez, "U.S. Exports of Advanced Technology Products to China", U.S. International Trade Commission, October 2009.)

[88] Computer equipment has risen particularly sharply, from $8.25 billion in 2000 to $43.1 billion in 2009.

[89] Derek Scissors, "US-China Trade Numbers Reveal Political Risk", The Heritage Foundation, February 14, 2011.

[90] "Some U.S. analysts have expressed concern over the composition of U.S. exports to China, noting that much of it consists of scrap products and components, as opposed to high value assembled products. They contend that restrictive Chinese trade practices and industrial policies have a major impact on the composition of U.S. exports to China. Chinese officials counter that U.S. export controls on high technology significantly reduce potential U.S. exports to China." (Wayne Morrison, *China-U.S. Trade Issues*, Congressional Research Service, Washington, DC, January 2011, p. 4.).

[91] Joanna Bonarriva, Michelle Koscielski, and Edward Wilson , "Export Controls: An Overview of their Use, Economic Effects, and Treatment in the Global Trading System", Office of Industries: U.S. International Trade Commission, August 2009, p. 1.

[92] Christopher F. Corr and Jason T. Hungerford, "The Struggles of Shipping Dual-Use Goods to China", January– February 2010 chinabusinessreview.com, p. 45.

[93] Wendell Minnick, "U.S. Eases Restrictions on Dual-Use Exports to China", Defense News, 01/19/09.

[94] "Rep. Markey Slams New Export Rule Favoring Chinese Company," Wisconsin Project on Arms Control, June 10, 2009. *http://www.wisconsinproject.org/pubs /editorials/2009 /markeyslamsnewrule-061009.htm.*

[95] Doug Palmer, "Chinese students press Locke on U.S. export controls", Reuters, May 21, 2010.

[96] Secretary Gary Locke, Remarks to BIS Update Conference, Tuesday, August 31, 2010, Grand Hyatt, Washington D.C.

[97] Hans Nichols and Gopal Ratnam. "Obama Wins Praise for Export Controls Overhaul", Bloomberg Businessweek, 09 September 2010.

[98] Otto Kreisher, "Obama Revamps U.S. Export Restrictions, Licensing", *National Journal*, December 9, 2010.

[99] Kevin L. Kearns, "Selling China the digital rope to hang us: Our advanced products can threaten national security", *Washington Times*, 01 March 2010.

[100] The U.S. is China's second largest pharmaceuticals importing partner behind Germany, and the "U.S. has been and will be China's largest pharmaceutical trade partner for a long time, as China is aimed to become the world's largest pharmaceutical outsourcing hub, with a focus on North American and European markets." See: *Potential Health & Safety Impacts from Pharmaceuticals and Supplements Containing Chinese-Sourced Raw Ingredients*, report produced by NSD BioGroup LLC on behalf of the U.S. China Economic and Security Review Commission, April 2010, p. 17, *http://www.uscc.gov/researchpapers /2010/NSDBIOPharmaReport--RevisedFINALforPDF-- 14 %20April 2010.pdf.*

[101] "Basic chemicals are used primarily in industrial and agricultural applications. These substances are used in producing plastics and agrichemicals as well as synthetic rubbers and fibers, detergents, pharmaceuticals, adhesives, inks, dyes and explosives. Resin, Synthetic Rubber and Artificial Synthetic Fibers and Filaments are mainly used in plastics tied to

packaging and consumer markets, construction materials, and automotive parts." (Georgia Power, "The Chemical Industry in Georgia", http://www.georgiapower.com/grc/pdf /chemical last accessed February 18, 2011.)

102 Pesticides, fertilizers and other agricultural chemicals made up 27.6 percent of chemical exports in 2000 ($637 million), but only 3.1 percent in 2009 ($369 million).

103 The share of transportation equipment among all exports from the United States to China declined slightly, from 12.5 percent in 2000 to 11.6 percent in 2010,

104 U.S. Department of Commerce, "Flight Plan 2011: Analysis of the U.S. Aerospace Industry," March 2011. http://trade n_2011.pdf

105 Michaela Platzer, "U.S. Aerospace Manufacturing: Industry Overview and Prospects", Congressional Research Service, December 3, 2009, p.1.

106 Aerospace products and parts have gone from 87.5% of transportation equipment exports ($1.8 billion) in 2000 to 54.3% ($5.8 billion) in 2010. Motor vehicles have risen from 2% of transportation equipment exports ($40.9 million) in 2000 to 33.1% ($3.5 billion) in 2010.

107 U.S. Commercial Service, "Aviation: Industry Overview", accessed February 18, 2011, *http://www.gbmabc.com*

108 Boeing Corporation, "China Market – a 10-Year Reflection." *http://www.boeing.com /commercial*

109 Xin Dingding, "Aviation Sector Has High Hopes for Next 5 Yrs", *China Daily*, February 25, 2011.

110 Peder A. Andersen, "China's Emergent Military Aerospace and Commercial Aviation Capabilities," Testimony before the U.S.-China Economic and ecurity Review Commission, May 20, 2010.

111 HS 8800 or 8802.

112 Steve Hargreaves, "Cashing in on a China Bet", CNN Money, January 25, 2011.

113 *IB Times*, "China confirmed $19 billion agreement with Boeing", January 20, 2011. "The large commercial aircraft fleet comprises 55 percent Boeing airplanes and 43 percent Airbus airplanes. Most of the remaining 2 percent are McDonnell Douglas aircraft produced before McDonnell Douglas's merger with Boeing." (Roger Cliff, Chad J. R. Ohlandt, and David Yang, "Ready for Takeoff: China's Advancing Aerospace Industry", Rand sponsored by the U.S.-China Economic and Security Review Commission, p. 6.)

114 *IB Times*, "China confirmed $19 billion agreement with Boeing", January 20, 2011.

115 Roger Cliff, Chad J. R. Ohlandt, and David Yang, "Ready for Takeoff: China's Advancing Aerospace Industry", report produced by the RAND Corporation on behalf of the U.S.-China Economic and Security Review Commission, p. 19. See also Wayne Morrison, *China-U.S. Trade Issues*, Congressional Research Service, Washington, DC, January 2011, p. 6.

116 James McGregor, "China's Drive for 'Indigenous Innovation': A Web of Industrial Policies", APCO, p. 34.

117 Therefore, rather than seeing air and rail travel as a zero sum game, the real question is whether or not the Chinese economy (and in particular, currently economically underdeveloped and under-visited geographic regions of China) will continue to develop at or near current rates.

118 "Ready for Takeoff: China's Advancing Aerospace Industry", Rand, Sponsored by the U.S.-China Economic and Security Review Commission, pp. 19-21.

119 Boeing's manufacturing policies also play a critical role in high exports of Boeing airplanes from the United States to China. "Boeing doesn't have a single manufacturing facility in China. While the company imports parts from around the world, including China, its planes

are assembled in the United States." (Steve Hargreaves, "Cashing in on a China Bet", CNN Money, January 25, 2011.)

[120] Thomas M. Hout and Pankaj Ghemawat, "China vs the World: Whose Technology Is It?", *Harvard Business Review*, December 2010.

[121] Robert Samuelson, "China's new world order demands stronger U.S. response", The Washington Post, January 24, 2011, drawing upon Thomas Hout and Pankaj Ghemaway in the *Harvard Business Review*.

[122] Roger Cliff, Chad J. R. Ohlandt, David Yang, "Ready for Takeoff: China's Advancing Aerospace Industry," RAND Corporation, 2011.

[123] Robert Samuelson, "China's new world order demands stronger U.S. response", The Washington Post, January 24, 2011. David Barboza, Christopher Drew, and Steve Lohr. "G.E. to Share Jet Technology With China in New Joint Venture", The New York Times, January 17, 2011.

[124] "GE Aviation is best known for its gas turbine engines, but its purchase of Smiths Aviation in 2007 signaled an intent to be as strong in commercial avionics. Smiths plays a major role on the 787 as the builder of the common core computing system, but its reputation is as an avionics supplier, not a prime manufacturer. GE's purchase of Smiths was to build it up to become a prime contractor; its partnership with Avic is the means to that end. For Avic, teaming with GE is a means to the end of establishing the Chinese company's importance in avionics manufacture. The emphasis on civil projects is intended to get past U.S. export control regulations." (Michael Mecham, "GE, Avic Sign Deal With Goal Of Dominating Avionics Market", *Aviation Week*, January 25, 2011.)

[125] "General Electric is counting on a joint venture with Avic to propel the company into the front ranks of avionics suppliers, just as its 50-50 partnership with France's Snecma turned CFM International into a powerhouse engine maker. With Chinese President Hu Jintao and U.S. Commerce Secretary Gary Locke looking on, GE Aviation President and CEO David Joyce and Avic Senior VP Zhang Xinguo signed an agreement Friday [January 21, 2011] in Chicago to form a joint venture—GE-Avic Civil Avionics Systems Co., Ltd.—in Shanghai." (Michael Mecham, "GE, Avic Sign Deal With Goal Of Dominating Avionics Market", *Aviation Week*, January 25, 2011.)

[126] David Barboza, Christopher Drew and Stephen Lohr, "GE to Share Jet Technology with China in New Joint Venture," *The New York Times*, January 17, 2011.

[127] "China Aviation Industry Corporation (AVIC) is an ultra large state-owned enterprise and an investment institution, authorized and managed by the Central People's Government. It is reorganized from AVIC I and AVIC II. The AVIC group oversees a wide range of business units, including defense, transport aircraft, aviation engine, helicopters, avionics, electromechanical systems, general aviation aircraft, aviation research and development, flight test, trade & logistics and asset management. It has nearly 200 subsidiaries (branches) and over 20 listed companies with a total of 400,000 employees. AVIC was ranked 330th in the Global Fortune 500 for 2010. It was the first Chinese aviation industrial company to make it into the rarified league." (GE Aviation Press Release, "GE and AVIC Sign Agreement for Integrated Avionics Joint Venture", January 21, 2011, http://www.geaviation.com/)

[128] Clyde Prestowitz, "Can Immelt Serve Both Obama and GE?", *Harvard Business Review*, January 24, 2011.

[129] James McGregor, "China's Drive for 'Indigenous Innovation': A Web of Industrial Policies", APCO, p. 34.

[130] Steven Pearlstein, "Chinese follow same old script (and they get the punch line)", *The Washington Post*, January 18, 2011.

[131] Roger Cliff, Chad J. R. Ohlandt, and David Yang, "Ready for Takeoff: China's Advancing Aerospace Industry", Rand sponsored by the U.S.-China Economic and Security Review Commission, p. 41-42.

[132] Roger Cliff, Chad J. R. Ohlandt, and David Yang, "Ready for Takeoff: China's Advancing Aerospace Industry", Rand sponsored by the U.S.-China Economic and Security Review Commission, p. 43.

[133] Roger Cliff, Chad J. R. Ohlandt, and David Yang, "Ready for Takeoff: China's Advancing Aerospace Industry", Rand sponsored by the U.S.-China Economic and Security Review Commission, p. xii.

[134] Roger Cliff, Chad J. R. Ohlandt, and David Yang, "Ready for Takeoff: China's Advancing Aerospace Industry", Rand sponsored by the U.S.-China Economic and Security Review Commission, p. 5.

[135] Roger Cliff, Chad J. R. Ohlandt, and David Yang, "Ready for Takeoff: China's Advancing Aerospace Industry", Rand sponsored by the U.S.-China Economic and Security Review Commission, p. xii.

[136] Roger Cliff, Chad J. R. Ohlandt, and David Yang, "Ready for Takeoff: China's Advancing Aerospace Industry", Rand sponsored by the U.S.-China Economic and Security Review Commission, p. 10-11.

[137] According to the Department of Commerce's International Trade Administration, U.S. automobile vehicle exports to China totaled $1.02 billion in 2009 and rose to $3.4 billion in 2010 (a 332.5 percent increase). U.S. automobile parts exports totaled $937 million in 2009 and rose to $1.28 billion in 2010 (a 136.4 percent increase). See International Trade Administration, "Automotive (Vehicles and Parts) Trade Data, Imports and Exports of Automotive Equipment 2000-2010," http://trade ade_pdf.pdf.

[138] Democratic Leadership Council, "Auto exports to China are up six-fold this year", Trade Fact of the Week, September 29, 2010.

[139] Jerry Hirsch, "GM's China sales top U.S. total, a first for the automaker", Los Angeles Times, January 25, 2011.

[140] Wayne Morrison, *China-U.S. Trade Issues*, Congressional Research Service, Washington, DC, January 2011, p. 6.

[141] *The Economist*, "Hitting the brakes", January 1st 2011, p. 34.

[142] "Car registration in Beijing has increased to 4.8 million from 2.8 million since 2005, with 700,000 new cars registered in the last year alone. The boom has created massive traffic problems in China's capital. The Chinese government now limits the number of new license plates in Beijing to 240,000 awarded annually through the lottery system." (Jerry Hirsch, "GM's China sales top U.S. total, a first for the automaker", Los Angeles Times, January 25, 2011.)

[143] "[GM] vehicle sales in China rose nearly 29 percent last year to 2.4 million, [while] U.S. sales rose just 6 percent to 2.2 million. Toyota Motor Corp., which narrowly beat out GM last year to hold its position as the world's largest auto seller, trails far behind its American rival in China, where the Japanese company sold 846,000 vehicles in 2010." (Jerry Hirsch, "GM's China sales top U.S. total, a first for the automaker," *Los Angeles Times*, January 25, 2011.)

[144] "GM sold more cars and trucks in China than it did in the U.S. last year, marking the first time that a foreign market has outpaced the automaker's domestic sales in its 102-year history. 'This is the wave of the future," said George Magliano, an economist at IHS Automotive.

"The Chinese market is going to grow faster than the U.S., and it will continue to be this way.'" (Jerry Hirsch, "GM's China sales top U.S. total, a first for the automaker", Los Angeles Times, January 25, 2011.)

[145] For example, "GM said [January 22, 2011] that it had signed a two-year agreement worth $900 million to export Cadillac, Buick and Chevrolet vehicles and components to China." (Jerry Hirsch, "GM's China sales top U.S. total, a first for the automaker", Los Angeles Times, January 25, 2011.)

[146] "A senior Ford Motor Co. executive said [on Friday, January 21, 2011] that the auto maker is in preliminary talks with Chinese authorities about exporting more North American-built vehicles to China's fast-growing domestic market... Ford on Friday signed an agreement with China's Ministry of Commerce as a first step in the planned export push... Last year, Ford sold 530,000 vehicles in China, a 40 percent increase over 2009. Most of the vehicles were assembled in domestic plants. 'We're looking to complement our Chinese vehicles with vehicles from the U.S.,' Mr. Biegun [vice president of International Governmental Affairs for Ford Motor Company] said." (Rob Tita, "Ford Aims to Export More to China", *The Wall Street Journal*, January 21, 2011.)

[147] Chang'an Ford Automobile Co., Ltd. is the joint venture between Ford Motors and China's Chang'an Automobile (Group), and Shanghai General Motors Company Ltd. is the joint venture between General Motors and China's Shanghai Automotive Industry Corporation (SAIC).

[148] Rachel Tang, "The Rise of China's Auto Industry and Its Impact on the U.S. Motor Vehicle Industry", *Congressional Research Service*, November 16, 2009.

[149] Rachel Tang, "The Rise of China's Auto Industry and Its Impact on the U.S. Motor Vehicle Industry", *Congressional Research Service*, November 16, 2009.

[150] *Ibid.*

[151] U.S.-China Economic and Security Review Commission, *2010 Report to Congress* (Washington, D.C.: November 2010), pp. 21 and 28.

[152] Doug Palmer and Lucia Mutikani, "China Yuan a Subsidy, Needs to Rise—Bernanke," Reuters, July 21, 2010, cited by U.S.-China Economic and Security Review Commission, *2010 Report to Congress* (Washington, D.C.: November 2010), p. 21.

[153] C. Fred Bergsten, "Beijing is Key to Creating More U.S. Jobs," Foreign Policy, April 14, 2010, cited by U.S.-China Economic and Security Review Commission, 2010 Report to Congress (Washington, D.C.: November 2010), p. 21.

[154] U.S.-China Economic and Security Review Commission, *2010 Report to Congress* (Washington, D.C.: November 2010), p. 29; see William Cline, "Renminbi Undervaluation, China's Surplus, and the US Trade Deficit", Peterson Institute for International Economics, August 2010.

[155] Geoff Dyer, "China Under Growing Currency Pressure," Financial Times, April 21, 2010, cited by U.S.-China Economic and Security Review Commission, *2010 Report to Congress* (Washington, D.C.: November 2010), p. 21.

[156] Daniel J. Ikenson, "China and Currency Valuation", *National Review (Online)*, March 17, 2010.

[157] Daniel J. Ikenson, "China and Currency Valuation", *National Review (Online)*, March 17, 2010.

[158] "U.S. officials, senators and some economists have predicted that if China allows the value of the yuan to rise, it will mean a smaller trade deficit with China, more American exports and more jobs for American workers. Fat chance on both counts, according to the American Chamber delegation... For one, the stuff China sells us has been imported by the United

States from other countries for decades. So if we don't buy it from China, we'll buy it from someone else. Take TVs. Twenty years ago, they all said "Made in Japan" on the back. Now they say "Made in China." If China allows the yuan to appreciate, it's not like TV manufacturing is going to move back to the United States and RCA Victor will rise anew. Americans will just buy them from someplace else." (John Pomfret, "China's industrial policy is bigger concern than yuan, U.S. executives say", *The Washington Post*, May 7, 2010.)

[159] "China's bureaucrats have been rolling out an array of interlocking regulations and state spending aimed at making their country a global technology powerhouse by 2020. The new initiatives—shaped by rising nationalism and a belief that foreign companies unfairly dominate key technologies—range from big investments in national industries to patent laws that favor Chinese companies and mandates that essentially require foreign companies to transfer technology to China if they hope to sell in that market.. 'It's a huge, long-term strategic issue,' says a top executive at a U.S. technology firm operating in China. "It isn't just the crisis of the day for U.S. business. It's the crisis." Deluged by complaints from companies, the U.S. Chamber of Commerce... commissioned a report to measure the scope of China's actions. It found what it calls... an 'intricate web' of new rules 'considered by many international technology companies to be a blueprint for technology theft on a scale the world has never seen before.'" (John Bussey, "U.S. Firms, China Are Locked in Major War Over Technology", *The Wall Street Journal*, February 2, 2011.)

[160] "An example? China used to import close to 100 percent of its wind-power turbines. Now it makes close to 75 percent of those that are sold in China. Chinese firms haven't developed wind-turbine technology; they've just required that foreign firms selling turbines in China share that technology, and now their firms manufacture the turbines at a lower cost." (John Pomfret, "China's industrial policy is bigger concern than yuan, U.S. executives say", *The Washington Post*, May 7, 2010.)

[161] John Pomfret, "China's industrial policy is bigger concern than yuan, U.S. executives say", *The Washington Post*, May 7, 2010.

[162] "According to the U.S. Census Bureau, U.S. imports of advanced technology products (ATP) from China in 2009 totaled $89.7 billion. ATP products accounted for 30.3 percent of total U.S. imports from China, compared with 19.2 percent ($29.3 billion) in 2003. In addition, China in 2009 accounted for 29.8 percent of total U.S ATP imports, compared with 14.1 percent in 2003." (Wayne Morrison, *China-U.S. Trade Issues*, Congressional Research Service, Washington, DC, January 2011, p. 7).

[163] "Over the past few decades, many multinational firms have integrated China into their global production networks by moving labor-intensive processing plants to the country for export purposes. It is often neglected, however, that these processing plants heavily rely on imported inputs for their exports, while only a relatively small portion of the export value is produced in China. In the media and even in academic and policy circles, this has led to important misinterpretations of China's role in the world economy." (Alyson C. Ma, Ari Van Assche, "China's Role in Global Production Networks", p. 19).

[164] Wayne Morrison, *China-U.S. Trade Issues*, Congressional Research Service, Washington, DC, January 2011, p. 8.

[165] U.S. Taiwan Business Council, "Semiconductor Report: Annual Review 2010", p. 7.

[166] Sylvain Plasschaert, "Is the Renminbi Undervalued? The myths of China's trade surplus and global imbalances", Ecipe Working Paper, No. 02/2011.

[167] "Processing exports [i.e. exports made using duty-exempt imported inputs] are more important in higher technology categories than in lower technology categories. In 2007, processing

exports accounted for 84.9% of high-technology exports; 45.6% of medium-high-technology exports; 26.6% of medium-low-technology exports; and 29.8% of low-technology exports." (Alyson C. Ma, Ari Van Assche, "China's Role in Global Production Networks", p. 4).

[168] U.S.-China Economic and Security Review Commission, *Hearing on Chinese State-Owned Enterprises and U.S.-China Bilateral Investment*, testimony of Dr. Theodore H, Moran, March 30, 2011.

[169] "In the mid-eighties, the Chinese government put [a] customs regime into place to entice foreign firms to offshore their production activities to China. Under this regime, firms located in China are granted duty exemptions on imported raw materials and other inputs as long as they are used solely for export purposes. Since its installment, processing exports has rapidly expanded to more than half of China's overall exports." (Alyson C. Ma, Ari Van Assche, "China's Role in Global Production Networks", p. 2). While this regime may have enticed foreign investment, it has also likely reduced government revenue from this investment, as this means that potentially significant portions of assembled exports are made using tax-free inputs.

[170] U.S.-China Economic and Security Review Commission, *Hearing on Chinese State-Owned Enterprises and U.S.- China Bilateral Investment*, testimony of Dr. Theodore H, Moran, March 30, 2011.

[171] U.S.-China Economic and Security Review Commission, *Hearing on Chinese State-Owned Enterprises and U.S.- China Bilateral Investment*, testimony of Dr. Theodore H, Moran, March 30, 2011.

[172] Alyson C. Ma and Ari Van Assche, "China's Role in Global Production Networks", p. 15

[173] Wayne Morrison, *China-U.S. Trade Issues*, Congressional Research Service, Washington, DC, May 6, 2011, Summary.

[174] Daniel Ikenson, "China Trade and American Jobs", Cato Institute, April 2, 2010. According to Dr. Moran, a similar study of Apple's iPhone conducted in 2010 by Yuqing Xing and Neal Detert" found that the value-added in China for the iPhone was $6.50 per unitm which was 3.6 percent of the total shipping price of the phone." (U.S.-China Economic and Security Review Commission, *Hearing on Chinese State-Owned Enterprises and U.S.-China Bilateral Investment*, testimony of Dr. Theodore H, Moran, March 30, 2011.) Supporting Ikenson's statement about the creation of U.S. jobs, Dr. Moran also notes that "US-headquartered MNCs have 70 percent of their operations, make 89 percent of their purchases, spend 87 percent of their R&D dollars, and locate more than half of their workforce within the US economy.... Thus, while manufacturing MNCs may build plants in China... the largest impact from deployment of worldwide earnings is to bolster their operations in their home markets." (U.S.-China Economic and Security Review Commission, *Hearing on Chinese State-Owned Enterprises and U.S.-China Bilateral Investment*, testimony of Dr. Theodore H, Moran, March 30, 2011.)

[175] Greg Linden, Jason Dedrick and Kenneth Kraemer, "Innovation and Job Creation in a Global Economy: The Case of Apple's iPod", *Personal Computing Industry Center*, January 2009, p.3.

[176] Greg Linden, Jason Dedrick and Kenneth Kraemer, "Innovation and Job Creation in a Global Economy: The Case of Apple's iPod", *Personal Computing Industry Center*, January 2009, p.4.

[177] Clyde Prestowitz, "Clyde Prestowitz: The Betrayal of American Prosperity (Excerpt)", May 11, 2010, http://www.progressivereader.com/?p=58997.

[178] Greg Linden, Jason Dedrick and Kenneth Kraemer, "Innovation and Job Creation in a Global Economy: The Case of Apple's iPod", *Personal Computing Industry Center*, January 2009.

[179] *The Economist*, "Multinational manufacturers Moving back to America", May 14, 2011. See also Gary P. Pisano and Willy S. Shih, "Restoring American Competitiveness", *Harvard Business Review*, July-August 2009.

[180] Andy Grove, "How America Can Create Jobs", *Bloomberg Businessweek*, July 1, 2010. For a much more positive account of the role of Chinese R&D in the scaling operations of multinational corporations and its effect in freeing their resources to focus on higher-value innovation, see Edward Steinfield's book *Playing Our Game: Why China's Rise Doesn't Threaten the West* (Oxford University Press, August 2010),

[181] "Research by the International Labour Organisation suggests that Chinese wages have been outpacing the rest of Asia for at least a decade. Chinese workers received real wage rises averaging 12.6 per cent a year from 2000 to 2009, compared with 1.5 per cent in Indonesia and zero in Thailand..." (Kevin Brown, "Rising Chinese wages pose relocation risk", Financial Times, February 15, 2011.) "Economists believe that China has hit a point in its development at which demand for labor starts to grow faster than supply, pushing up salaries. A survey conducted by Standard Chartered in the first quarter of 2011 showed average wages in a sample of 87 manufacturing firms rising by 9 percent to 15 percent from the previous year." (Jason Dean and Tom Orlik, "China Signals Yuan May Be Inflation Tool", *Wall Street* Journal, April 21, 2011.) ""Guangdong Province, the export heartland of light industry next to Hong Kong, announced [in January 2011] that its cities were raising their minimum wages [again] by an average of 18.6 percent, effective March 1..." (Keith Bradsher, "Inflation in China May Limit U.S. Trade Deficit", *The New York Times*, January 30, 2011.)

[182] "The shortage of migrant workers that gripped the Pearl River Delta region and the coastal areas of Fujian Province in 2003 gradually seeped its way into the Yangtze River Delta region and other coastal provinces. In 2009, this trend extended to several cities in central China.... "Labor shortage" and the upward trend in wages for migrant workers indicate that the transfer of rural surplus labor in China may have reached a turning point, changing from an infinite supply to a finite surplus. A shortage of the young labor force is beginning to emerge." (Jianmin Li, "China's Looming Labor Supply Challenge?", The Jamestown Foundation, China Brief Volume: 11 Issue: 6, April 8, 2011.)

[183] "...manufacturing experts doubt that many high-tech companies are planning to abandon China – not least because many rely on suppliers who have co-located in southern China's vast technology clusters specifically to be near their customers. Bhavtosh Vajpayee, head of technology research at CLSA in Hong Kong, says: 'It is not possible for these high-tech companies to shift much of their production to Asean countries; they just don't have the skills and the infrastructure that is needed. It just cannot be done.'" (Kevin Brown, "Rising Chinese wages pose relocation risk", *Financial Times*, February 15, 2011.)

[184] "The higher Chinese prices will tend to show up mainly in products like inexpensive clothing and other commodity goods in which labor and raw materials represent a bigger part of the final value — rather than in sophisticated electronics like Apple iPads, in which Chinese assembly is only a small fraction of the cost." (Keith Bradsher, "Inflation in China May Limit U.S. Trade Deficit", *The New York Times*, January 30, 2011.)

[185] "Coach, the American company that is one of the largest marketers of luxury handbags and other accessories, announced on Tuesday that it planned to reduce its reliance on China to less than half of its products, from more than 80 percent now. It will shift output to Vietnam and India, particularly for smaller, more labor-intensive leather goods", though this will

likely take about 4 years according to the company's executive vice president and chief financial officer. (Keith Bradsher, "Inflation in China May Limit U.S. Trade Deficit", *The New York Times*, January 30, 2011.) See also John Gapper and Barney Jopson, "Coach to shift manufacturing from China", Financial Times, May 12, 2011

[186] "Matt Rubel, chief executive of Collective Brands, the US footwear group that owns the Payless shoe stores chain, is shifting a chunk of production from China to Indonesia, south-east Asia's largest economy. 'The utopia for one stop sourcing for quality and low price has been China . . . but utopias never last,' says Mr Rubel." (Kevin Brown, "Rising Chinese wages pose relocation risk", *Financial Times*, February 15, 2011.)

[187] Jianmin Li, "China's Looming Labor Supply Challenge?", The Jamestown Foundation, China Brief Volume: 11 Issue: 6, April 8, 2011.

[188] Feng Wang, "China's Population Destiny: The Looming Crisis", Brookings, September 2010.

[189] Jianmin Li, "China's Looming Labor Supply Challenge?", The Jamestown Foundation, China Brief Volume: 11 Issue: 6, April 8, 2011.

[190] U.S. International Trade Commission, "China: Intellectual Property Infringement, Indigenous Innovation Policies, and Frameworks for Measuring the Effects on the U.S. Economy", November 2010, p.1-2.

[191] U.S. Census Bureau, "Advanced Technology Product Definitions" (Washington, DC: U.S. Department of Commerce, July 12, 2011), http://www.census.gov/foreign-trade

[192] Alexander Hammer, Robert Koopman, and Andrew Martinez, "China's Exports of Advanced Technology Products to the United States", U.S. International Trade Commission, October 2009.

[193] U.S. Census Bureau, "U.S. International Trade in Goods and Services" http://www.census.gov /foreigntrade/Press-Release/current_press_release/exh16a.pdf.

[194] Elliot Musilek, "A Closer Look At U.S.-China Trade in Advanced Technology Products", Center for Strategic and International Studies, August 18, 2010.

[195] Alexander Hammer, Robert Koopman, and Andrew Martinez, "U.S. Exports of Advanced Technology Products to China", U.S. International Trade Commission, October 2009.

[196] For an account of China's "dramatic, unexpected, and unplanned reversion toward heavy industrial production" starting in 2002, see Matthew Ferchen, "China–Latin America Relations: Long-term Boon or Short-term Boom?", *The Chinese Journal of International Politics*, Vol. 4, 2011, pp. 75, 79-81.

[197] Another major Chinese import which has not been examined in this report is machinery, much of which (especially high-end machinery) China imports from Germany's *Mitelstand.* While machinery is also a top manufactured export from the U.S. to China, the U.S. has an overall trade deficit with China in terms of machinery. (See Figure 12) U.S. machinery exports to China jumped from around $6.5 billion in 2009 to $9.3 billion in 2010.

[198] U.S.-China Economic and Security Review Commission, *Hearing on Chinese State-Owned Enterprises and U.S.- China Bilateral Investment*, testimony of Dr. Theodore H, Moran, March 30, 2011.

[199] In January 2011 "Bloomberg New Energy Finance, a research group, reported that investors had injected a record $243 billion into cleaner sources of energy in 2010... Investment in clean energy in China rose 30 percent last year, to $51.1 billion - by far the largest figure for a single country - and represented more than 20 percent of the total global investment..." (James Kanter, "China, Once Suspect on Emissions, is Rapidly Becoming a Clean-Energy Power", *The New York Times*, January 26, 2011.)

[200] In 2009, three of the ten largest wind turbine manufacturers in the world were Chinese — Sinovel, Goldwind, and Dongfang. (John Acher, "China became top wind power market in 2009: consultant", *Reuters*, March 29, 2010.)

[201] China has been the largest solar cell producer since 2008. In 2009, four of the ten largest photovoltaic cells and modules producers in the world were Chinese — Suntech Power, Yingli, JA Solar and Trina Solar. (Hirshman, W. P., "Surprise, surprise (cell production 2009: survey)," *Photon International*, March 2010, pp. 176-199.)

[202] This category includes computer hardware.

[203] This category includes computers.

INDEX

C

D

E

F

G

J

K

L

M

N

O

P

T

U

V

W